# MORE SERMONS
# I SHOULD LIKE TO
# HAVE PREACHED

edited by
IAN MACPHERSON

FLEMING H. REVELL COMPANY
WESTWOOD, NEW JERSEY

# CONTENTS

5

# PREFACE

He who preaches a dull sermon commits a crime. These are strong words, but not too strong. To give the impression by one's mode of presenting it that the most wonderful message in the world, a message on whose acceptance the eternal destinies of men depend, is a dry, drab, lacklustre, boring affair is to be guilty of an offence the gravity of which it would be impossible to exaggerate.

Yet who will deny that countless sermons *are* dull? The phrase 'Dull as a sermon' has passed into a proverb. And the tragedy is that so many people – preachers and hearers alike – have come to assume that that is how things must continue and that nothing whatever can be done about it.

Not *all* sermons are dull. Certainly not those in this collection! And practical steps *can* be taken by anyone who has a mind to it to improve the standard and the state of his preaching! Let the minister who suspects himself of pulpit dullness – and who of us does not at times do that? – adopt as models for his own the discourses in this compilation; let him study their structure and style, their methods of introducing, stating, outlining, developing, illustrating and applying the truths of which they treat, and he is not likely to incur the charge of falsifying and misrepresenting his high theme by heavy handling of it.

The warm and wide welcome extended to the Editor's

previous volume, *Sermons I Should Like to Have Preached*, has led him to venture on this further anthology. He hopes that the new collection will similarly commend itself to the Christian reading public.

I.M.

# WHAT IS VITAL IN LIFE

## G. T. BELLHOUSE

*And it is my prayer that your love may be more and more
rich in knowledge and all manner of insight, enabling you
to have a sense of what is vital.*

Philippians 1⁹⁻¹⁰

'Enabling you to have a sense of what is vital.' So Dr
Moffatt translates the rendering of the Authorized
Version: 'That ye may approve things that are excellent',
and what a much more vivid translation it is! For 'to
have a sense of what is vital' is one of the most important qualifications any of us can have. Upon its
possession depends our chance of success in any walk
of life.

In scholarship, in politics, in teaching, in preaching,
what lifts one man high above his rivals, who remain
ordinary and ineffective, is his sense of what is vital,
his ability to pierce through to the central thing and
go straight for it. It is the same with a young person's
study, his preparation for and sitting of an important
examination. Again and again why some fail or just
scrape through is that they seem to have little sense of
what is vital in a question and waste their time in
irrelevancies. It is the same in the building of a successful business. Here to succeed a man must have a
sense of what is vital, vital in the siting of the business,

11

in the choosing of assistants, in the stock carried, in advertising. It is, of course, supremely true in the life of the Church. Can you wonder that many today consider the Church utterly irrelevant to life as they know it? The endless discussions that churchmen indulge in about minutiae of belief, of orders, of worship. In Thomas Hardy's novel, *Jude the Obscure*, Jude and Sue are sitting in their bare room at Oxford utterly broken-hearted by the death of their child. Their taut nerves are further stung by the sound of voices in argument in the street outside. Distractedly, Jude goes to the window to listen, and reports: 'It's just two clergymen of different views arguing about the eastward position.' It's a cruel touch of Hardy's, but not altogether unjustified. Just as tragically irrelevant to many must sound some of the discussions of churchmen.

It is the same with the whole living of life. Here it is essential that from the very outset we have a sense of what is vital. Living a life is like building a house. We have only a certain amount of space, a certain amount of material. We must not waste it on long, draughty passages, and neglect the living-room, the kitchen, and the scullery. So it is with life. We have only a certain amount of time, a certain amount of material. We must concentrate on the essential things, on what really is vital.

What, then, is vital for a true living of life?

*First, surely, a right philosophy of life, a true reading of the facts, a right interpretation of what they are all about.*

Those facts often seem such a dreadful jumble. There is much happiness and loveliness in life, but there is also much pain and sin and suffering. The older we get, the shorter life seems, and death comes to us all. What does it all mean? What are we here for, if for anything? Some say it means nothing. 'Some vast Imbecility, mighty to build and blend, but impotent to tend, hath framed us in jest and left us to hazardry.' Others say: 'Don't bother your head. "Gather ye rosebuds while ye may" and take what you can get.'

But there comes times when we do cry out desperately: What does it all mean? What is it all about? And so often we utter that cry too late. The storm is upon us and we don't seem able to think. We need to think it out before the storm comes. What, then, is the meaning of life? It certainly has not been originally designed as a pleasure-cruise or as a trading company where all the dividends that are honestly earned are fairly paid. No! Life in its deepest sense is a school of manhood, a 'vale of soul-making'.

'Considered as a dance,' wrote the late Canon Streeter, 'life is an entertainment which doesn't come off. Other people do the steps all wrong, the band gets out of tune; the material conditions which make the dancing floor are seldom smooth, and our toes get sore. But think of life not as a dance, but as a battle, and wounds and weariness are what we should expect. They hurt, but do not dishearten. They may exhaust, but will not embitter.'

In other words, the meaning of life is that we are here on a pilgrimage; we are here to grow a soul, through all life's experiences of joy and sorrow to get closer to God and to one another, to view every fresh challenge as another examination to be passed, and

death, when it comes, will be the entrance into life
more abundant.

*The second thing that is vital for a true living of life is a
right view of ourselves, and consequently of what are the
right values to strive for.*

Schopenhauer, the distinguished German philosopher,
who spent half a lifetime brooding on the mystery of
existence and never could make up his mind who man
was and why he was here, was sitting one day in the
Tiergarten at Frankfurt when the park-keeper, disliking
his dishevelled appearance and thinking him a tramp,
accosted him and said: 'Who are you?' The philosopher,
interrupted in his reverie, looked up and said with awful
earnestness: 'I wish to God I knew!'

Well, who are or what are we?

The first thing that is obvious about all of us is that
we are such strange, tantalizing mixtures.

*Within my earthly temple there's a crowd:*
*There's one of us that's humble, one that's proud;*
*There's one that's broken-hearted for his sins,*
*There's one who, unrepentant, sits and grins;*
*There's one who loves his neighbour as himself,*
*There's one who cares for nought but fame and pelf –*
*From much corroding care I should be free*
*If once I could determine which is me.*

How very true those lines are! There is a weak, slack,
preferring-the-easy-way-to-the-hard-way side of us. It
is what the Church means when it speaks about human
nature as 'fallen'. But there is another side to us, a
Godlike side, and we only find blessedness as we take

that lower side and seek to fashion it into the image of the higher: as we take the sex instinct and control it and build it into a love that is fine and clean and enduring; as we take the power instinct, the desire to get on, to achieve a place, and consecrate it to the service of a better world. We were never meant to be just the victims of our instincts, still less of our temperaments. How often people seek to excuse themselves on the ground that that is the way they have been made! But others made the same way win the victory. As Maude Royden once said: 'Our temperaments may decide our trials, they need not decide our destinies.' That is, they may determine the particular way we are tested, but they need not decide the result of that testing. That depends on us and our power to say 'Yes' or 'No'. It is that word 'discipline' which we need to get back into our vocabulary today. 'We are,' wrote Paul to the Corinthians, 'God's field to be planted, God's house to be built.' We are, that is, the raw material out of which something fine is to be made.

A friend once told me of hearing, so that he never forgot, the late Dr Sangster crying to his great congregation at the Westminster Central Hall: 'You may have lost your way. But don't lose your address!' That address is God and the heavenly country.

Once in a discussion about the atomic bomb, C. S. Lewis is reported to have said: 'And, anyhow, just when the bomb falls there always will be a split second in which one can say: "Pooh! you're only a bomb. I'm an immortal soul!"'

This is the essential truth about each one of us. We are immortal souls. We may lose our way. We must never lose our address.

*The third thing that is vital, and the most important for the true living of life, is a continuing sense of God.*

Amiel began his famous *Journal* with the words: 'There is but one thing needful – to possess God.'

How very true that is! Only so do our standards remain right. Lose religion, lose God, as this age is in danger of doing, and you lose all sanctions, all standards, and morals lapse into chaos.

Only so do we get the power to live as in our finest moments we know we ought to live.

> *Grant us the will to fashion as we feel,*
>   *Grant us the strength to labour as we know,*
> *Grant us the purpose, ribb'd and edged with steel,*
>   *To strike the blow.*

Only so do we get a centre to our lives. So many people's lives today are like a clock which has lost its pendulum, just a mass of whirring wheels, fruitlessly consuming and wasting energy, and the so common nervous breakdown results. But attach the pendulum to that clock, and the result is a movement which is peace – stable, restful, calm, purposeful. What has happened? The law of gravitation has come into play, and that clock has been taken up into the mighty movement of the universe, the movement which rules the tides and the stars. It is as we go into the silence and quietly wait upon God that our little lives are taken up into the rhythms of the universe and given poise and peace.

And it is only as we are aware of God that we feel really at home in life. 'It's curious,' said Dr Micklem to Dr Farmer, as they came away from a service in Oxford, 'what a feeling of settled completeness, of final rounded-offness, worship, and worship alone, gives to life.'

'A sense of what is vital!' Get it early. Never depart from it. This life was designed by God to be lived in a certain way. You see it all in Jesus. Stay close to Him and His saints.

# THE PERFECT WORKER

## G. N. M. COLLINS

*The pleasure of the Lord shall prosper in His hand.*
Isaiah 53¹⁰

This familiar chapter leads us along the *Via Dolorosa* to Calvary, just as surely as do those passages in the Gospels which record the final scenes of our Lord's humiliation and suffering. The central figure in the narrative is Jehovah's Suffering Servant, about whose identity so much has been written. Some regard him as the embodiment of the Jewish nation in the suffering of the Captivity. Others identify him as Cyrus, whom Jehovah indeed designates as His servant in the respect that he was used by God for the liberation of His captive people. And there are others who award the title to Isaiah himself, or to Jeremiah.

But we are not left in the region of conjecture in this matter; for this was the passage of Scripture over which the Ethiopian eunuch was puzzling when Philip, by the direction of the Holy Spirit, joined himself to his chariot. 'I pray thee,' asked the eunuch, 'of whom speaketh the prophet this? Of himself? Or of some other man? Then Philip opened his mouth, and began at the same Scripture, and preached unto him Jesus' (Acts 8³⁴⁻³⁵).

It is with this authoritative identification in mind

that we proceed to consider this reference to the Suffering Servant.

*Let us consider the work described.*

'The pleasure of the Lord' – what does it mean? Clearly, the work assigned to this Servant was one that was to involve Him in suffering; for the verse begins: 'Yet it pleased the Lord to bruise Him.' But why, *why?* For 'He had done no violence, neither was any deceit in His mouth. Yet it pleased the Lord to bruise Him.'

In some of the ethnic religions the gods are represented as deriving pleasure from the sufferings of their devotees; but we can never associate such a thought with the God and Father of our Lord Jesus Christ. When Moses, in the awesome solitude of the mount, prayed: 'I beseech Thee, show me Thy glory,' God said: 'I will make all My goodness to pass before thee', and proclaimed Himself as 'the Lord, the Lord God, merciful and gracious, longsuffering, and abundant in goodness and truth, keeping mercy for thousands, forgiving iniquity, transgression and sin, and that will by no means clear the guilty' (Exodus 34[6-7]).

There was indeed a background of judgement: the character of God would be less than holy were it otherwise. But, shining like a cluster of stars against that sombre background were God's attributes of mercy and grace. These were the qualities by which God most desired to make Himself known to sinful men, and this was no newly-assumed attitude on His part. For if He did come to Eden on the day of man's fall to reprove his sin and proclaim his punishment, He came also to make the first announcement of saving grace; in the promise that there should come of the seed of the woman the Victor who should bruise the head of the serpent and, necessarily, be bruised Himself in the process.

In various ways God reveals where His pleasure concerning a sinful humanity lies. His forbearance, for instance, reveals it. For if His pleasure had lain in the immediate punishment of sin there was nothing to hinder the execution of His purpose. He could have justly hurled the thunderbolts of His wrath at the sinner in the very moment of his transgression, had He so pleased. But He delayed, not because sin had taken Him unawares, or that He was confronted with an unforeseen situation and was uncertain as to how it ought to be met. By the stay of judgement He was giving man time and opportunity to repent and be saved. How tenderly He pleads with Ephraim in the prophecy of Hosea! Backsliding, incorrigible Ephraim was ripe for judgement, but God was slow to inflict it. 'How shall I give thee up, Ephraim?' He cries; and who can measure the yearning of His words? 'How shall I deliver thee, Israel? How shall I make thee as Admah? How shall I set thee as Zeboim? Mine heart is turned within Me, My repentings are kindled together' (Hosea 11[8]).

This long forbearance in face of great and continued provocations shows where His pleasure lies. For even in His times of wrath – holy and deserved wrath – He remembered mercy. He laid man under a curse because of his sin, but not without telling him of the way of escape. He threatened to destroy the ancient world with a flood, but for four hundred years He stayed His judgement while Noah proclaimed his message of mercy and pointed men to the refuge which God Him-

self had provided. 'Say unto them,' was His charge to
Ezekiel, and the reference was to a people who were
wringing judgement from His hand, 'As I live, saith
the Lord, I have no pleasure in the death of the wicked;
but that the wicked turn from his way and live: turn ye,
turn ye, from your evil ways; for why will ye die, O
house of Israel?' (Ezekiel 33[11]).

Again, God's provision for man's salvation reveals
what the pleasure of the Lord is. By the institution of
sacrifice He showed that salvation was suffering,
vicarious suffering, the sufferings of His own Son, 'the
Just for the unjust, that He might bring us to God.'

What a fine understanding of the pleasure of God
was revealed by Manoah's wife in that well-known
story in Judges! An angel of God had appeared to her
to announce that she was to bear a son who was to
become Israel's deliverer from their oppressors. At the
entreaty of Manoah, the angel returned and repeated
the message. But, when the messenger departed,
ascending to heaven in the flame of the altar, Manoah
was filled with consternation. 'We shall surely die,' he
cried, 'because we have seen God.' But his wife did not
share his alarm. 'If the Lord were pleased to kill us,'
she reasoned, 'He would not have received a burnt-
offering and a meat-offering at our hands, neither
would He have showed us all these things, nor would
He, as at this time, have told us such things as these'
(Judges 13[23]).

Her logic was irresistible, especially when related to
the Cross. For if God had desired our death, why the
Cross? If His pleasure lay in man's punishment, why
the sin-offering of Calvary? His provision of our
salvation is the final argument of His mercy. 'He par-

doneth iniquity,' cries the Old Testament prophet, 'and passeth by the transgression of the remnant of His heritage; He retaineth not His anger for ever, because He delighteth in mercy' (Micah 7[18]). And how intense that delight is we may gather from the teaching of Christ Himself, especially in Luke 15 – 'the Lost and Found column of the New Testament', as it has been described. The restoration of the lost sheep, the recovery of the lost coin, the return of the lost son were such joyful events that the finders decided to multiply their happiness by sharing it with their neighbours. And the lesson that the three parables have in common is 'there is joy in the presence of the angels of God over one sinner that repenteth.'

*More particularly, let us now consider the difficulties involved.*

The expression 'taking a thing in hand' has a familiar meaning. We understand it as denoting the undertaking of a task, the accepting of a duty. So what the prophet is telling us here is that Christ took in hand the salvation of His people. 'And the pleasure of the Lord,' he exclaims, 'shall prosper in His hand.'

And yet, how improbable it all seemed! Think of the difficulties which He had to face.

First of all, man's guilt was already established. In our law courts the guilt or innocence of a person committed for trial is a matter of argument between opposing counsel. Guilty he may indeed be, but, unless his guilt can be established by the evidence led, he will have to be discharged. But no such possibility exists for any transgressor of God's law. The evidence is conclusive. The sinner stands in the presence of an omniscient

Judge. 'Thou hast set our iniquities before Thee,' cries Moses, 'our secret sins in the light of Thy countenance.' He shall 'bring every work into judgement, with every secret thing' (Ecclesiastes 12¹⁴).

Furthermore, man's guilt is beyond excuse. It sometimes happens that, even after the guilt of an accused person has been established, room is left for leniency because of certain mitigating circumstances in the case. The plea may be that the offender acted under strong provocation, or under the pressure of some compelling need, or in association with a character stronger than himself, or that he had an unfortunate domestic background. But, although every age has brought its own inventions, such a thing as a valid excuse for sin has never been devised. And, although it is as natural for man to sin as it is for him to breathe, the fact of his fallen nature cannot be accepted as a plea for mercy. The law is explicit. 'The soul that sinneth, it shall die' (Ezekiel 18⁴).

Nor must it be overlooked that *the sentence of the divine law is unappealable*. In our legal system, if a case is lost in a lower court, it can be taken by appeal to a higher one. But, condemned as he is by the High Court of Heaven, to which tribunal shall the sinner direct his appeal? 'It is God that justifieth,' writes Paul, 'who is he that condemneth?' (Romans 8³³⁻³⁴). But suppose the case were otherwise! Suppose God condemned: who then could justify?

Never did a pleader undertake a more difficult case; and yet, it was to 'prosper in His hand'. For His intercession was to be based upon the perfect obedience of His life and the perfect atonement of His substitutionary death.

There is a wonderfully bright gleam of Gospel truth in the law regarding the impoverished Jew who, under the pressure of his need, sold himself into the service of the rich stranger. 'After that he is sold' – so runs the enactment – 'he may be redeemed again; one of his brethren may redeem him' (Leviticus 25⁴⁸).

The qualifications of the redeemer were three in number. He must be a *kinsman;* he must be willing; and he must be sufficiently rich to accomplish the redemption. These three qualifications of Redeemership are clearly evident in Christ. He became our Kinsman to become our Redeemer. The eternal Word 'was made flesh and dwelt among us' (John 1¹⁴). And He was rich, 'yet for your sakes He became poor,' writes Paul, 'that ye through His poverty might be rich' (2 Corinthians 8⁹). And He was willing. As the Kinsman-Redeemer, under the law of Israel, was subject to no obligation save that of his own compassion, so too was Christ. He laid down His life of Himself: no man took it from Him (John 10¹⁸). And because He fulfilled the conditions so perfectly there could be no doubt as to the consequence.

*Finally, then, we consider the result anticipated.*

'The pleasure of the Lord shall prosper in His hand.'

He is the perfect Servant with whom there can be no failure. His finished work is adumbrated in that of Zerubbabel, the royal temple-builder. The besetting difficulties were so many and so great that it seemed the building must remain an incomplete and useless monument to the zealous but futile endeavours of a great patriot. Yet in face of this apparently impossible situation the words of the prophet rang out challengingly:

'The hands of Zerubbabel have laid the foundation of this house, his hands shall also finish it' (Zechariah 4⁹). The building of the temple was 'the pleasure of the Lord' and it was to 'prosper in his hands'.

It was in the certain prospect of a finished work of redemption that our Lord claimed in His great inter-cessory prayer: 'I have glorified Thee on the earth; I have finished the work which Thou gavest Me to do' (John 17⁴). The claim was repeated a little later in the cry from the Cross in which is concentrated the very essence of the Gospel: 'It is finished!' (John 19³⁰). The pleasure of the Lord had prospered in His hand!

And the sufferings, the humiliation, the shame endured shall be regarded as compensation by the results, which He sees in part even now. 'He shall see of the travail of His soul,' exults the prophet, 'and shall be satisfied' (Isaiah 53¹¹). For, by bearing 'the sin of many', the Righteous Servant shall 'justify many' (Isaiah 53¹¹⁻¹²).

How inexpressibly comforting is it to God's people to know that their affairs are in such capable and loving hands! It was a fine tribute that Naomi paid to Boaz when Ruth told her that her new-found friend, Boaz, had undertaken to play the part of kinsman-redeemer to them. At the hearing of these tidings, the fears and anxieties of the older woman were completely banished. 'Then said she, Sit still, my daughter, until thou know how the matter will fall; for the man will not be in rest until he have finished the thing this day' (Ruth 3¹⁸).

That was the kind of man Boaz was. When he took a thing in hand, he never rested until he had carried it to completion. And that, precisely, is what the prophet is telling us here about the Suffering Servant of Jehovah. He never leaves a thing unfinished. Where He begins a good work, He carries it on to perfection. When He finishes, there is nothing more to be done. It was the certainty of this fact that led Hudson Taylor into the joy of salvation. 'There dawned upon me,' he testifies, 'the joyous conviction that, since the whole work was finished and the whole debt paid upon the Cross, there was nothing for me to do but to fall upon my knees, accept the Saviour and praise Him for evermore.'

A minister, who took more than usual pains with the Christian instruction of his family, was questioning them one evening after family worship. The reading had been the story of the Passover in Exodus 12. How had it come about, he asked, that Death, which had entered the homes of the Egyptians, had been halted at the dwellings of the Israelites? He had expected the reply that the Israelites were protected by the sprinkled blood of the Paschal lamb, but the answer – which came from the youngest member of the family – showed far greater penetration. 'Death', she said, 'could not enter there, because Death had been there already!'

She was right! The blood upon the door-posts and the lintels was but the outward sign of the people's trust in a propitiation which had already been made. Death had received his due and had no further demand to make. It is that fact which secures the believer. By the death of his Substitute, God's Suffering Servant, the claims of justice have been met, the wages of sin have been paid. The death which was required for the remission of sins has taken place, so that the believer can say with confidence:

*If Thou hast my discharge procured,*
*And freely in my stead endured*
   *The whole of wrath divine,*
*Payment God will not twice demand,*
*First at my bleeding Surety's hand,*
   *And then again at mine.*

With our salvation entrusted to such strong, capable hands, we can say with Paul: 'I am not ashamed: for I know whom I have believed, and am persuaded that He is able to keep that which I have committed unto Him against that day' (2 Timothy 1[12]).

# THE SIN OF PRAYERLESSNESS

## George B. Duncan

*God forbid that I should sin against the Lord in
ceasing to pray for you.*    1 Samuel 12[23]

It is important to recognize that sin can be of two kinds.
Sin consists either in the doing of what I know to be
wrong – 'Sin is the transgression of the law' (1 John 3[4]);
or sin is the failure to do what I know to be right – 'To
him that knoweth to do good, and doeth it not, to him
it is sin' (James 4[17]). We call these, theologically, sins of
commission and sins of omission. Both are sins; and it
is questionable whether it is worse to be a man who does
the worst, or one who fails to do the best. Possibly
such are equally sinners in the sight of God.

One of the most common, most serious, sins in
Christian living is the sin of prayerlessness. 'God forbid
that I should sin against the Lord in ceasing to pray for
you.' This failure is one which involves every Christian,
for prayer is possible to every child of God. We cannot
all preach – and some of us who think we can, do not
do too well at it! But we can all pray. We cannot all
give large sums of money, although most of us could
give more than we do. We cannot all go to the mission
field. We cannot all witness in the open air. We cannot
all lead a meeting for Bible study. But we can all pray,
in the privacy of our room or in the corporate act of

28

prayer in the life of our church. This we can all do. This we all ought to do. Indeed we are promised help for this very thing if we feel that we need it.

One of the very first evidences of life is a cry, and one of the first marks of the new life is a prayer. The sin of prayerlessness! I wonder how common this failure is.

Andrew Murray recalls addressing a gathering, and the question was asked how many spent thirty minutes in prayer a day. One hand went up. How many spent fifteen minutes in prayer a day? Not half the hands went up. How many spent five minutes in prayer a day? All the hands went up; but afterwards one came to say that he did not know if he even spent five minutes a day in prayer. In contrast to this is the witness of the history of the Church, that whenever God works it is in answer to prayer.

So I want to examine and think over the question: 'Wherein is prayerlessness sin?' I believe this is something to which far too many of us have become far too accustomed.

*I suggest to you that prayerlessness is sin, first, because by prayerlessness the Cross of Christ is despised.*

I say this because I find that one of the characteristics, one of the privileges of the Christian life has to do with that access to God which we are meant to enjoy.

Sometimes Christians have argued as to which is the true symbol of the Christian faith – a cross or a crucifix. Without going into the answer to that question, which might be controversial, I should like to point out that the first symbol of the Christian faith and its significance was neither. The first symbol was the rent veil of the temple; rent from the top to the bottom, rent by the hand of God, announcing to mankind that the very essence of the Christian experience that was now to be available to man, was the access that men could now enjoy into the very presence of God Himself; a symbol of the fellowship now possible between a holy God and a sinful man.

And in this connection I want us to note two things.

First, the untold price of this access. The veil of the temple was rent in twain only when the price was paid for our redemption. It was only when Jesus cried with a loud voice and gave up the ghost that the veil of the temple was rent in twain from the top to the bottom. It is this access which includes the privilege of prayer; and this was bought at infinite cost, the infinite worth of the Son of God.

This is surely what the writer to the Hebrews has in mind when he says: 'Having boldness to enter into the Holiest by the blood of Jesus, by a new and living way, which He hath consecrated for us, though the veil, that is to say His flesh, let us draw nigh.' Again, St Paul writes: 'Being justified by faith, we have peace with God through our Lord Jesus Christ, by whom we have access.' Such was the untold price paid by God that we might have the right to come into His very presence.

And when I think of the untold price, I find myself looking at the untrod path. The price has been paid, but the path is so seldom used. How hurtful this must be to the heart of God! What despite we do to the Cross when we fail to take advantage of the privilege it has bestowed upon us!

Prayer is spoken of by Christ as one of the normalities of the Christian life. You recall His words in

Matthew 6⁶: 'When thou prayest', not, 'If thou prayest.'
Christ assumes that His people will pray and that,
first of all, in secret behind a closed door. His teaching
extended to include a praying together: 'If two of you
shall agree on earth as touching anything ye shall ask,
it shall be done for them of My Father which is in
heaven' (Matthew 18¹⁹). The Early Church practised
this togetherness in prayer from Pentecost on. The
access is meant to be used. The privilege is meant to be
valued. The gift is meant to be treasured. The untrod
path does despite to the untold price. And every time
we neglect the path, we despise the Cross which opened it.

Is it any wonder, then, that we speak of the sin of
prayerlessness – to treat the Cross in such a way? Have
you ever thought of it like that? Or have you thought
of the sin of prayerlessness as simply a kind of slackness
and spiritual laziness? I suggest to you that prayerlessness is sin, because in prayerlessness the Cross of Christ
is despised. Is that not an awful thing to say? But is
it true?

*Secondly, I submit that prayerlessness is sin because by
it the Church of Christ is deprived.*

I gather this from the fact that not only is there an
access the Christian is meant to enjoy in prayer, but
that there are answers the Christian is meant to receive
in prayer. Nothing is clearer from both Scripture and
history than that prayer does something; or, if you
prefer it, prayer enables God to do something. We sing
our hymn:

> *Prayer moves the arm that moves the world,*
> *To bring salvation down.*

Or, if we are in the chorusing brigade, we sing: 'Prayer changes things.' And if the hymn writer is right and the chorus writer is right, then presumably the absence of prayer means that things are not changed and that the arm is not moved.

Let us, then, take note of the encouragement of the Word of God to prayerfulness. We find these both in Scripture and in experience. Here we face a commonplace statement, when we say that the Bible is full of promises. It is a fact that it is so; although we must not overlook the other fact that conditions are imposed as well. There is nothing unconditional about praying. 'If I regard iniquity in my heart, the Lord will not hear me,' says the Psalmist (Psalm 66[18]). The unrepentantly sinful will not be heard. The rebel is out of court. 'Ye ask and receive not, because ye ask amiss, that ye may consume it upon your pleasures' (James 4[3]). This reminds us that purely selfish prayer is unacceptable to God. Prayers not in the name of Jesus, not in harmony with the character of Jesus, not in line with the will of God – these will find no response.

But, granting all that, and much more besides – recognizing that God's answer may be 'Yes' or 'No' or 'Wait', or that God's answer could be what we need rather than what we want – encouragements to prayer abound in the Bible. 'Ask, and ye shall receive; seek, and ye shall find; knock, and it shall be opened unto you. For every one that asketh receiveth, and he that seeketh findeth, and to him that knocketh it shall be opened' (Luke 11[9-10]). Our God is presented to us as the One who hears and answers prayer. And still we do not pray.

Think of the encouragement to prayerfulness;

think of the impoverishment of prayerlessness. 'Ye have not,' says James, 'because ye ask not' (James 4²). Somehow I feel that this could be written across almost every Christian's life, every church, yes, even across a convention for the deepening of spiritual experience. 'Ye have not, because ye ask not.' When the resources are there, and they have never been tapped – is not this a sin?

Try to catch this vision for a moment. God has placed each of us Christians at the centre of ever-expanding circles of contact, contact with human needs that only divine grace could meet – of which need we may well be the only Christians with any knowledge, within the circle of our homes and relations, within the circle of our street and our neighbours, within the circle of our church and its members, within the circle of our work and our workmates and colleagues. Each of us is a circle with circles of contact, ever-expanding circles; and we are the only Christians with any knowledge and contact. I began by quoting: 'Ye have not, because ye ask not'; I think we could write that almost as accurately and as truly: 'They have not, because we ask not.'

Oh, the impoverishment through prayerlessness! Is it any wonder that the Bible speaks of prayerlessness as a sin? Prayerlessness is a sin because by it the Cross of Christ is despised and the Church of Christ is deprived.

*And I want to suggest one other reason why prayerlessness is a sin – because by it the cause of Christ is defeated.*

I say this because I find in the aspects of the Christian life that are set out in the Word of God, not only is there this access that we are meant to enjoy, not only are there these answers we are meant to receive, but there is also this attack that we are meant to defeat.

'Upon this rock I will build My Church', says Jesus Christ, 'and the gates of hell shall not prevail against it' (Matthew 16[18]). And right through the New Testament there is the language of battle and conflict. In Ephesians 6[12-18], Paul reminds us of the spiritual conflict upon which we are engaged, and his description of the Christian's armour ends with a reference to what John Bunyan called the weapon of 'All-Prayer'. 'Praying always with all prayer and supplication in the Spirit, watching thereunto with all perseverance and supplication for all saints' (v. 18). And this passage recalls another author in 2 Corinthians 10[3-4]: 'Ye do not war after the flesh, for the weapons of our warfare are not carnal, but mighty through God.'

Think for a moment of the warfare in which we are engaged. Let us never forget that we are up against spiritual forces of evil. 'We wrestle not against flesh and blood, but against principalities, against powers, against the rulers of the darkness of this world, against spiritual wickedness in high places' (Ephesians 6[12]). If that language of the stately old version sounds a bit unreal, does this help you? 'Our fight is not against any physical enemy; it is against organizations and powers that are spiritual. We are up against the unseen, the power that controls this dark world, and spiritual agents from the very headquarters of evil.'

We are in a battle, a battle against spiritual forces in conflict against which human weapons are powerless and futile. And if there is warfare in which we are engaged, there are the weapons with which we are equipped – and among them the weapon of All-Prayer.

Fancy going into battle without your equipment! We have so much in trust that to go into battle without our equipment, without a vital part of it, is to go into defeat. It is indeed to be defeated before the battle has commenced. When you and I talk about being defeated, we are very often thinking in terms of some moral capitulation or some evangelistic failure. Do not some of us even think that we are pretty good Christians? We have quite a good record behind us; we know all the answers; we have all the language; we could stand up and give a Bible study on any subject. And all the time we are defeated Christians. We are defeated here.

Is your church a defeated church? Wherever the Church lives victoriously, it fights prayerfully. When revival swept the church of Robert Murray McCheyne in Dundee, do you know how many prayer meetings were going on in that church during the week? Thirty-nine prayer meetings, five of them attended by children alone! How many prayer meetings are there in your church and in mine, and how many at them: are you at them at all? Maybe you cannot go every week, but you could go more often than you do. You see, there is an attack that we are meant to defeat. You and I are meant to win, not to lose.

When Christ rose on Easter morning, it was a triumph; it was a victory. Yet that note of victory and triumph, that sense of advance and achievement, has almost died right out of our Christian thinking today.

I had in my hands the other day the book telling the story of Lillias Trotter of North Africa, and one little sentence stood out challengingly to me. It was this: 'Fighting does not mean standing up and being hit.'

Somehow or other, you know, I think that is just about all that some of us are doing. We are just standing up as Christians and being hit. People, everyone, is hitting us; and we are not making any advance. There is no sense of conflict, no note of achievement. We are just being hit by everyone, and we think we are great stuff, standing there being hit.

No! we are not just to be hit. True, there will be wounds in battle; there always are. There are sometimes casualties, and in warfare they are usually treated with kindness: in the Christian Church, usually with contempt! There will be wounds; there will be casualties; there will be hurts. But there ought to be advance; there ought to be achievement; the enemy ought to be being defeated.

I think that possibly the reason why he has not been overcome as he should have been is that all the time far too many of us have been guilty of the sin of prayerlessness.

Somebody said once that the real sins of the Christian Church are those that the world would not reckon to be sins. The world does not see anything wrong in a man who never spends a minute in prayer. The world does not think anything ill of a man like that. But what does God think? Possibly some of the greatest sinners in God's sight are those who are guilty of the sin of prayerlessness.

# THE WIND OF THE SPIRIT

## R. A. Finlayson

*The wind bloweth where it listeth, and thou hearest the sound thereof, but canst not tell whence it cometh, and whither it goeth: so is every one that is born of the Spirit.*

John 3[8]

It was our Lord who most frequently drew attention to the close connection between natural and spiritual law, a connection that was to Him inevitable and inescapable since the one God was the author of both.

For that reason He used the most commonplace of natural phenomena to illustrate the most mystical spiritual experiences, and to cast light upon the hidden operation of the Spirit of God.

There is, for example, that well-known illustration of His, which forms our text, and which is concerned with the working of the Spirit of God in the regeneration of the human soul: 'The wind bloweth where it listeth, and thou hearest the sound thereof, but canst not tell whence it cometh, and whither it goeth; so is every one that is born of the Spirit.'

Here our Lord clearly teaches that there are attributes of the wind in its operation that are analogous to the workings of the Holy Spirit of God, and He indicates what they are. They are three, and we might do well to take them to heart in these days of spiritual dearth and spiritual unrest, when the minds of earnest Christian people seem to oscillate between despair of any genuine spiritual revival visiting the land, and a feverish agitation to do something to produce that revival themselves.

Taking the wind as the natural agency that guides us to a clearer perception of the operations of the Spirit of God, we note these simple facts.

*The wind cannot be controlled, but it can be used.*

'The wind bloweth where it listeth' and so cannot be controlled or interfered with in its course. It is a sovereign influence and none can temper or change or soften it in its course. This quality of the wind has remained unchanged with the passing of the years, and unaffected by the advance of human knowledge.

On the other hand, it is equally true that while neither the wise man nor the fool can control the wind, both use it to their own advantage. If we give obedience to the laws of the wind, we may make it serve us and bless us. We can set our sails to catch the breeze and it drives us either out to sea or into port. Whither the wind drives depends on the set of the sails, and a skilled mariner can sail in the teeth of the wind.

In like manner there are spiritual processes, as our text suggests, that cannot be controlled; but they can be made use of to our lasting good. We are not disposers of our own lot; the Father of spirits has perfect control of those spiritual processes within us that affect us so deeply and may change us so radically. In many an unwilling breast there stirs a movement toward spiritual realities which we cannot control. We may resist and oppose it and try to stem it, but we shall find it as irresistible as the wind, since it is the moving of the life-giving Spirit of God.

Let us not try to smother the rising concern within our breasts, lest we be found to resist the Holy Ghost. Rather let us use it to our eventual peace and blessedness.

As with individuals, so with nations. 'The wind bloweth where it listeth.' In His nation-wide movements the Holy Spirit is not subject to man's control. One era He blows softly over Asia, another over Europe, another over America, and yet another over the distant islands of the sea. Truly, in all His operations the Holy Spirit is like the wind which 'bloweth where it listeth'.

May it be ours to set our sails to catch the first fresh gust of wind that alone produces that 'forward movement' that our human organization has sought to produce in vain! And even when the wind blows from unexpected quarters, may we be skilled mariners that can sail in the teeth of the wind and be driven by many strange and apparently harsh providences into havens of spiritual security and peace.

*The wind cannot be seen, though it can be heard.*

That is the second quality of the wind we note from our text. 'Thou hearest the sound thereof' is our Saviour's comment. Though heard, the wind is invisible.

There is an element of secrecy about the wind. No one has ever seen it. The keenest eye cannot see it, nor can it become visible through the telescope or under the microscope. But it can be heard. It has a distinctive sound as it rushes through the trees of the forest. We can see the mighty monarchs of the forest bend under its influence and sometimes break before its gale. Thus the *sough* of the wind is known to us all; we have heard it whistle to every tune and on every key, while it remains itself invisible.

So are the movements of the Spirit of God. Spiritual processes, as a rule, cannot be seen. There is a great mystery about the divinest things in life. God's mightiest forces are secret forces. God's greatest works are operations in which the hand of the Worker is hid.

But though God's greatest forces are unseen, they may often be heard; they find expression in language that becomes audible and intelligible. For example, the life that is under the regenerating and sanctifying power of the Spirit of God is a life that speaks. Great lives have been known to bend before the breeze and they gave forth an unwonted sound. Sometimes they sighed like the wind among the trees of the wood, sometimes they gave forth music like the Aeolian harps of the Black Forest. On the day of Pentecost, when the Holy Spirit came like a mighty rushing wind, every man in the motley crowd heard the apostles speak in his own tongue. When the Holy Spirit of God is in direct contact with men, we shall hear them speak in our own tongue, in a language that our hearts and consciences can understand, the language of conviction, of pardon, of peace and grace. Thus we claim that spiritual processes are secret in their operation, but not in their results. They produce lives that speak.

*The wind cannot be understood, but it can be experienced.*

That is the third quality of the wind which our Lord mentions. 'Thou canst not tell whence it cometh and whither it goeth' points to our complete ignorance. The way of the wind is wrapped in mystery, and we are still very ignorant of the laws that govern it. Though we speak in technical terms of 'depressions' and such like, the fact remains that atmospheric movements are very much a mystery to us.

Yet, though we do not understand the way of the wind, we can experience its blessings. It brings to us the clouds that carry the rain and the breath that cools the fevered brow. It brings to us the very life that we constantly breathe. Yet we confess that we 'do not understand whence it cometh or whither it goeth'. Shall we not believe in the wind because we do not fully understand it? Shall we cease to use it because we do not comprehend it? Since we do not understand the composition of the atmosphere or know the origin and destination of the wind, shall we refuse to breathe it? Surely not!

In like manner we do not profess to understand the life-giving processes of the Spirit of God; but we experience them and, therefore, we fully believe them. We are called to believe and experience many things we do not fully understand. Though our religion is not unnatural, it is supernatural, and it stretches far beyond our present comprehension. There is mystery in our religion before which man must stand with bared head and unshod feet. Yet we can live within that mystery and experience its regenerating and sanctifying power. In other words, though there are things in our religion beyond our comprehension, they are not for that reason outside our experience. There are glorious and profound mysteries in our Gospel which we do not fully understand, yet they are having a profound influence upon our hearts and lives.

The central fact of the Gospel message – the Incarnation – is beyond our present powers of comprehension, and it seems to us an event in which, to quote a mystic of last century, 'nature stood aside to let God pass'. But we are not for that reason to question its reality. Indeed, to the Christian heart it has been through the ages the pillar of hope and the great source of comfort.

Other truths there are in our most holy faith which we cannot fully understand, but which we can experience in their reality of light and comfort and peace. 'Thou canst not tell' may be written over many of our most deeply-cherished articles of faith, but we shall not cease to cherish them for the reason that we have had experience of their truth and their power.

Thus simply stated these are facts so patent as to be almost self-evident. Yet the holding of them in memory would keep us from those extremes in evangelism which characterize so much of our Christian effort – the extreme, on the one hand, of despair when we feel our helplessness in face of the task committed to us, and that of self-confidence, bordering on presumption, when we recognize the might of the instruments placed in our hands. We need this admonition at the present hour and there can be no surer corrective to black despair or a facile optimism than this consciousness of God's sovereignty in grace.

Let us contemplate this sovereignty of the gracious Spirit of God and then by faith take hold of His sovereignty as the only means by which we can wield power with God and with men. Then shall we recognize with gratitude and awe that the movements of the Spirit are like the wind, which cannot be controlled but can be used, which cannot be seen but can be heard, which cannot be understood but can be experienced.

# THE UNSHAKEN KINGDOM

## Donald MacLeod

*The kingdom we are given is unshakable.*
Hebrews 12$^{28}$ (NEB)

Adam Burnet, one-time minister of St Cuthbert's, Edinburgh, told of an experience he had during the First World War. He was standing one evening not far from the tall spire of a village church in France. For some unknown reason the firing on both sides of the line had died down and in the stillness he watched the setting sun like a great ball of fire upon the horizon. Suddenly a single shell came screaming through the twilight and the top half of the church steeple blew apart with a shocking roar. Almost simultaneously a flock of swallows, which had been nesting there, rose slowly above the smoke and flying debris, circled the air for a moment, and then settled back quietly upon the wreckage of where they had been. Burnet said that this reminded him of the greatness of God. After the world and life are shaken, and men have done their worst, God's greatness remains unshaken, unlimited, unimpaired.

I do not know how you, as individuals, are reacting to the crucial events and times through which we are now passing. It would sound trite for me to say that these are 'stirring and stormy' days; nevertheless, we are

43

cheered and encouraged when, here and there across
the land, someone squares his shoulders and declares,
in Dr Fosdick's phrase: 'It's a great time to be alive!'
But the alarming fact is that the number of people is on
the increase who are meeting today and tomorrow in a
spirit of fear, cynicism, and despair. Is it not a matter
of concern to you that tourists returning from abroad
say that the people of Britain and Europe go about
their business calmly and realistically, while here at
home so many of us are caught up in the climate of
uncertainty and dread? Indeed, we feel a slight chill
when, for example, someone begins to ask wistfully:
'Whatever happened to the American dream?' Is there
not something unhealthy in the temperament of our
people when an elderly lady observed recently and
cynically: 'This world won't be too difficult to leave
behind!' And there was the young man who said: 'I
couldn't care less. What's the future got to offer me
anyway?' And, again, John Oliver Nelson, formerly
of Yale, has reported that in many student groups
today an old slogan is being revived: 'Blessed is he who
expects nothing, for he will not be disappointed.'

Now it is true that these are not ordinary times.
Indeed, there is something dangerous and momentous
about these days, and anyone seeking only a part of
life's picture is liable to feel that we have all got our
backs against the wall. But, from the long perspective
of history, these times are not unique. We are not the
first generation of mankind to be caught in the whirl-
wind of revolution or in the maelstrom of the breaking
of nations. A mere glance at the index of time will
notice scores of occasions when it seemed that the earth
and heavens were being shaken and everybody was

listening to the counsels of despair. What grim and grave hours in the story of Man are suggested by such dates as the year 70 in Jerusalem, 410 in Rome, 1805 in England, 1914 in Europe, and 1941 in America! How appropriate in any one of these crises would be the words of the English statesman, John Bright, when he declared in the House of Commons over a century ago: 'The angel of death is abroad in the land; you can almost hear the beating of his wings!'

Without a doubt these, too, are days of shaking; indeed, this world cannot avoid being shaken, because change is written into the very constitution of life. For the Christian, however, the basic question has always to do with the fruit of change: Will this shaking produce a vacuum or a new creation? The Christian, moreover, believes that this is still God's world and that it is by His law that things are shaken; and therefore the hope of the hour rests with those who live by a spiritual order whose dimensions are most real when the fortunes of men and nations are most insecure. Indeed, human experience has shown us that, whenever men defy God's laws of truth and right, the laws themselves are not broken, but, as Chesterton remarked: 'Men break themselves against them.' Or whenever any of God's creatures are enslaved by social, economic, or religious bondage, sooner or later this tyranny must come to terms with man's will to freedom and his potential as a child of God. Or whenever men or nations come into the possession of tremendous power, sooner or later they will encounter a Sovereign Will above their own, to which inevitably they are held accountable. And if there is any lesson history has written large across our times, it is this: We live in a universe that is morally on the square and whenever this fact is flouted or ignored, there follows a violent shaking of human destiny, during which little people cry out in despair, while men and women of faith declare: 'The Lord God omnipotent reigneth!'

Consider the situation in the Scripture text before us. It was about 1,880 years ago when the writer of the Epistle to the Hebrews looked out upon the life and fortunes of the Early Church. He saw some people meeting the onslaught of persecution with steady endurance and resolute hearts; but some others were living to themselves and had lapsed from their earlier Christian commitment and were indifferent now to its claims. He warned these of an impending crisis when God would shake the things of time so that the timeless realities would emerge as the only true objects of human faith. Now, none of these – neither the loyal nor the disloyal – would escape God's testing of His world; but, for men of faith, there was an 'eye of calm' at the centre of the hurricane. 'The kingdom we are given is unshakable.' And, therefore, even in a day of violent change, the Christian always knows whose man he is: what commands his ultimate allegiance: in what he can honestly put his faith.

How are we to describe this kingdom for our times and what relevance does it have anyway?

*This kingdom is unshaken because it involves not a quantity of living, but a quality of life.*

Gerald Kennedy has told of a country girl who married a well-to-do boy from the city. After a while she wrote home to her mother to say that she had more nice clothes than she had ever had; she was meeting the kind of people she had always wanted to meet; and she was going to all the theatres she had time to attend. Then she added: 'There is only one thing wrong – I hate my husband!'

What a commentary on life! Yet, in a sense, is it not ours, too? Our emphasis is too often upon quantity – how much of this or that we have; and we list the things the Russians or Chinese or Africans do not have. And such a concern crowds out inevitably quality of life, and men become worshippers of quantity as an end in itself. Hence we do more getting than giving, more grasping than loving, and we are more bored than happy with all we have. Jesus said: 'The kingdom of God is within you.' And thereby He defined our highest moral and spiritual condition as 'the rule of God' in our hearts. And everyone who encountered Him felt the reality of this kingdom because Jesus Himself was the rule of God alive in their midst. Moreover, whenever anyone opened his soul to permit this rule of God to begin within himself, a violent and revolutionary shaking occurred among his aims and values and never again did he crave for quantity of living in preference to quality of life.

One day John Tauler, the fourteenth-century German mystic, met a beggar on the highway. As his custom was, he addressed him thus: 'God give you a good day, my friend!' But the beggar answered curtly: 'I thank God I have never had a bad day.' 'Well, then,' said Tauler, 'God give you a happy life.' But the beggar retorted again: 'I've never been unhappy.' 'What do you mean?' asked Tauler. 'Well,' said the beggar, 'when it is fine, I thank God; and when it rains, I thank God. When I have plenty, I thank God; and when I am hungry, I thank God. And since God's will is my will and since whatever pleases Him pleases me, why should I be unhappy?' 'Who are you anyway?' asked Tauler. 'I am a king,' came the reply. 'You, a king!' laughed Tauler, 'where's your kingdom?' 'In my heart,' whispered the man in rags, 'in my heart!'

You see: quantity of living is always in the area of outer achievement, while quality of life is something received within. Indeed the worst illusion we can hold today is to suppose that we can achieve our own destiny. You and I become what we are destined to be only through God's rule in our hearts. This kingdom alone can provide us with that new dimension that claims us from the fruitless levels of quantitative living. And, when we have it, we shall point to our homes with satisfaction, not for their comforts and gadgets, or all the products of our American 'know-how', but for that Christian love which holds us together and rides out the storms of sorrow, failure and disappointment. We shall point to our cities with joy, not for their skyscrapers and neon lights, but for the sensitive conscience and moral stability of their communities in the face of every violation of truth and right. And we shall point to our schools and colleges with pride, not for their strides in the technique of learning alone, but to generations of young men and women who know how to deal with life because the meaning of life is in their hearts.

*This kingdom is unshaken because it is not static but possesses creative power.*

When Jesus talked about the kingdom, it was not a matter of advising people to stand still and simply not to do certain things. Remember how proud the Rich Young Ruler was when he informed Jesus that he did not do this or that. But when Jesus challenged him with the daring and demanding adventure of the kingdom, he refused to have any part in it. For Jesus, this kingdom could never be an ingrown organization in which nothing creative ever happened or a place where people held on to the *status quo* lest their complacencies should be shaken. For Him this kingdom was an adventure; it was not for people who thought they had arrived: it was for those who would share in its growing power. Hence He challenged one man to sell all he had and give it to the poor; another to gamble everything he owned in order to win the pearl of great price; and eleven reluctant disciples to go out into a tottering world with nothing to support them except the promise of His presence. This kingdom is always on the move because its spirit is vital, dynamic, and venturesome. It turns up in the most unexpected places and asks the right questions about ourselves, about the way we live and the things for which we live.

And this is why some of the greatest gains for God's kingdom have been realized in times when all our little schemes and pet notions were being shaken to the foundations. Indeed one of the most determinative factors has been the attitude of many so-called good people in a period of shaking. Some think that, if they stand pat and motionless, the sharp issues and revolutionary movements of our times will either peter out or go away entirely. But this just isn't going to happen! The shaking of these days must be met by people who are so committed to the rule of God in their lives that it becomes in them the most thrilling and contagious cause they have ever known. And once they are caught up in it, they become the spearhead of those great purposes that mould human destiny. This is the only life that counts any more. You and I cannot go back to the old world; we cannot go back to the old world because the old world is no longer there. It has been shaken, not by men but by God, and He alone can give us that new creative power to equip us for service in the days to come.

Among the touching events in the life of Winston Churchill was his farewell visit to the House of Commons in 1964, where, sixty-five years earlier, he had come as a newly-elected member. Among the fine tributes paid to him on this occasion was one by a former prime minister, Harold Macmillan, who turned to the younger members of the House and said: 'However long you live, you will not see his like again.' In one sense this was a grand utterance; but, on second thought – how utterly pessimistic! Is the day of the great individual over? Is the day of the towering and inspiring personality gone for ever? Must we be led henceforward by the average fellow or inspired only by the least common denominator? I cannot speak for the world of politics, but what a sorry day such would be for the world of religion!

Some months ago another book among many others on Albert Schweitzer, *Verdict on Schweitzer*, was written by Gerald Knight. A review in the *New York Times* commented as follows: 'This faceless world of the twentieth century is not an age of heroes. This is the age of panels, commissions, opinion polls, mass movements, and the like. To those weary of the materialism of the West, repulsed by the totalitarianism of the East, searching for a human ideal to which they may pledge their soul, the image of Schweitzer has towered out of the black jungle of Africa to inspire and serve as an altar of dedication.' In these shaken times, how much we need great Christian personalities to rise up here and there across the life of the nation and the Church; to rise above the debris of worn-out methods and sterile structures, above the facelessness of the mass mind; and, like some holy purpose come alive, to permit God to live out His purpose afresh among us.

*This kingdom is unshaken because it belongs not to time but to eternity.*

Jesus said to Pilate: 'My kingdom is not of this world.' And Paul wrote to the Philippian church: 'Your citizenship is in heaven.' Although they were in the world, they were not of the world. Their lives and destiny were controlled by a spiritual order from beyond themselves. And Jesus was so convinced of the integrity and durability of this kingdom that Calvary itself was not too much to endorse this truth.

In Kennedy's play, *The Terrible Meek*, the centurion said to Mary at the foot of the Cross: 'I tell you, woman, that this dead Son of yours – disfigured, shamed, spat upon – has built this day a kingdom that can never die.' And Canon Liddon of St Paul's once said: 'Christianity alone, of all the systems of thought I have studied, gives me an answer to two of life's biggest questions: Who am I? and Where am I going? ' And this Christianity is the story of a kingdom that came alive in a Person whose very presence shakes your life and mine, but always redemptively.

But you ask: How can I get it? Or, you say: What is

the use of talking about an unshaken kingdom that seems so unreal, while we are jostled about and trampled upon by the mad forces of a shaken world? Well, you cannot get this kingdom because you cannot get a personal experience. But there is a way to begin and it is suggested by an old Gospel hymn we used to sing in our Sunday School days:

> *Simply trusting every day,*
> *Trusting through a stormy way;*
> *Even when our faith is small,*
> *Trusting Jesus, that is all.*

And this is too big a thing for any of us to be indifferent or sophisticated about it.

Late in the nineteenth century there lived in Scotland a distinguished Old Testament scholar named John Duncan. It was said that he was so expert in the Hebrew language that he handled it as freely as his own mother-tongue: indeed his colleagues had nicknamed him 'Rabbi' Duncan. It was a joke among his students that when the old man said his prayers at night he spoke to God in Hebrew rather than in English. One night two of the boys crept stealthily up to the old professor's bedroom door to hear if his petitions were offered in the Hebrew tongue. In the quiet they heard him kneel; and then softly and clearly through the door they heard:

> *Gentle Jesus, meek and mild,*
> *Look upon a little child;*
> *Pity my simplicity,*
> *Suffer me to come to Thee.*

This is where the unshaken kingdom begins. It appears in the little events and relationships of time, but it is grounded in eternity. But dare you face tomorrow without it?

# THE PSALM OF THE TWO WAYS

## George Campbell Morgan

*Jehovah knoweth the way of the righteous; but
the way of the ungodly shall perish.*    Psalm 1[6]

Dr Thirtle has called this 'The Psalm of the Two Ways',
and the aptness of that designation is patent. This
final verse summarizes all the teaching of the psalm.
The first movement – verses one to three – describes one
way, the way of the righteous. The second movement –
verses four and five – describes another way, the way of
the wicked. The last verse makes a declaration concerning these two ways.

The general idea of this psalm is common in biblical
literature. The Old Testament teaches it in the law,
enforces it in the prophets, interprets it in poetry, and
illustrates it in history. That idea may thus be briefly
stated: righteousness pays and wickedness does not;
and, therefore, righteousness is the secret of happiness
and wickedness the cause of misery.

That is an extremely old-fashioned idea, and it is
certainly out of date today. Yet that conception of life
was accepted generally by people born and brought
up in the light of the biblical revelation.

It was so accepted until the closing years of the
nineteenth century, and then it began to go out of
fashion. That general idea ran through all Shakespeare's

54

plays, and was interpreted in all fiction until the closing years of the nineteenth century. Shakespeare's plays all have a moral drift. Macbeth never escapes; Shylock must come to judgement. Always righteousness pays, wickedness does not. It is the fashion today to laugh at the old fiction in which people went through all sorts of processes, and married, and were happy ever after. That is not popular now. In the fiction I read in my youth, the villain always got his deserts before the book was done. He seemed to be very successful for a while, but he got run to earth at last. All that is out of fashion. Modern plays ignore it, and the general drift of modern fiction laughs at the idea that righteousness pays and wickedness does not; that righteousness is the secret of happiness and that wickedness is the cause of misery.

Well, it may at least be well to remind ourselves that old-fashioned ideas are not necessarily untrue and that newness is not a guarantee of truth. It is good occasionally to make a commonplace remark like that to help us in our thinking. It is the fashion now, if you want to dismiss anything, to call it Victorian. If a thing is Victorian, it is considered as something out of date. That does not prove it wrong. There may have been some very futile things in the Victorian age. I lived and was born and brought up in it, thank God, and all its influences are with me and will be to the end; and I know that there were in it some foolish things, some of them almost as foolish as some of the things mastering the thinking of men today.

But because a thing is old it is not necessarily wrong, and because it is new it is not necessarily right; and I am going to submit to you that in this matter the old is certainly the true, and all the new which contradicts it in philosophy and fiction, or in any other realm, is untrue to the facts of life.

This old singer in the Hebrew economy looked out on life, and he saw two ways of living which he has described for us, and described them with singular accuracy, pictorially and definitively; and he sums up the whole thing at last by saying: 'Jehovah knoweth the way of the righteous, but the way of the wicked shall perish'; or literally, as to the Hebrew word, 'The way of the wicked shall *run out*', the picture suggested being that of the track trodden by the cattle which presently is lost in the prairie. It runs out. Ultimately, it is not a way at all – it perishes. The way of the righteous is known to Jehovah: the way of the wicked runs out, leads nowhere, arrives nowhere. That is the summary of the singer.

Now let us first consider the two ways as they are here described, and then let us bring the description of the psalm to the test of experience.

*We will first take the way of the wicked.*

As to description, it comes last in the psalm, and yet it is referred to in the opening verses – 'the counsel of the wicked', 'the way of sinners', 'the seat of scoffers'. Let us examine these carefully chosen words. He speaks of the counsel of the wicked – *counsel;* the way of sinners – *way;* the seat of the scoffers – *seat.*

'The *counsel* of the wicked'. This word 'counsel' means advice, deliberation, finding, and so philosophy. The counsel is the philosophy of the wicked; that is, that which condones, justifies, or excuses wickedness.

Much of the literature which is being poured out upon us in this day is literature either justifying or condoning or defending or ignoring what our fathers called wickedness. That is the philosophy of the non-moral, or more accurately of the immoral. Every form of thinking or writing, whether in philosophic treatise or fictional representation or religious literature, which minimizes sin is the counsel of wickedness, the philosophy of wickedness.

'The *way* of sinners.' That is the road, the course of life, the activity, which harmonizes with the counsel – the way of sinners. All conduct is the outcome of conception. Man does nothing save as the outcome of his thinking. 'As a man thinketh in his heart, so is he.'

'The *seat* of the scoffers.' The word seat here means a session. The session of the scoffers, that is, their settled agreement, their unanimous position. The mental attitude of those holding the philosophy of the wicked is that of scoffing at goodness.

That is one way of life. Its philosophy, the denial of morality; its way, conduct that harmonizes with the denial; its seat, its session, its unanimity, scoffing at goodness.

That is a remarkably accurate diagnosis of the atmosphere of the hour in which we are living today. First of all, the philosophy of the age is condoning or justifying or ignoring sin; so that if a man writes the biography of Heine he will so do it as to suggest that all rotten corruption of the man was merely artistic expression. That way lies hell! This philosophy, the counsel of the non-moral, is producing the way of today, which is the way of sinners and of rampant wrongdoing. And at last there is general unanimity, and we hear those so influenced, and so acting, with unanimity laughing at goodness. In much brilliant journalism and clever literature and vulgar comic papers and scripts, of every chance to laugh at goodness advantage is taken.

Now, passing to the end of the psalm, let us see what this singer had to say about that way of life. He says: 'The wicked are like the chaff which the wind driveth away.' We only get the full impact of that statement when we observe the singer's contrast. Speaking of the righteous, he says: 'He shall be like a tree planted by the streams of water, that bringeth forth its fruit in its season.' Some day, when the wind blows up a hurricane, look at a tree planted, rooted, and then at some chaff! If you do, you will have caught the significance of this declaration concerning the wicked. Thank God, there are winds of God blowing all over human history, winds of God blowing today – trying, testing, sweeping winds; and they carry away the chaff. The wicked are not like the tree. 'The wicked are not so, but are like the chaff which the wind driveth away.'

Therefore, he says further, they 'shall not stand in the judgement'. Do not postpone the activity suggested by that word judgement. There is to be a great Assize, a Great White Throne, a great Day of Judgement: but judgement is already operating. We live every day in the presence of judgement. Judgement is discrimination, that which makes the difference between right and wrong. The wicked cannot stand in the judgement. There is a discrimination at work in the world and in human history. It is operating today, right here and now and everywhere – the discrimination which wickedness cannot bribe and cannot deceive. They 'shall not stand in the judgement'.

And, once again, 'Nor sinners in the congregation of the righteous'. That is, they are excluded from the gathering together of the righteous. Wickedness can get by a great many operations of so-called law. But wickedness cannot get by the eternal principle of discrimination, which is dividing sharply for ever between right and wrong; and the winds of God that sweep across history and human life are for evermore driving the chaff away. John the Baptist said of your Lord and mine, our blessed and adorable Redeemer, God's holy Son, the Son of Man: 'He shall come, and His fan shall be in His hand, and He shall gather the wheat into His garner, and the chaff destroy in the unquenchable fire.' That is the biblical outlook upon wickedness.

Now let us look at the other side. Here is another way: 'Blessed is the man that walketh not in the counsel of the wicked, nor standeth in the way of sinners, nor sitteth in the seat of the scoffers.'

This is a negative description of another man and another way of life. 'Walketh not' – that is, he refuses the philosophy; 'standeth not' – that is, he declines the activity; 'sitteth not' – that is, he denies the unanimity. The counsel of wickedness – this man refuses, denies, the philosophy. The way – resulting from the philosophy of sinners, this man does not go near it. He declines all the activity that comes out of the philosophy. There is a session of the scoffers, and the ribald laughter of the intellectuals who have dismissed God and goodness altogether; and is there a great unanimousness about it? No! There is not. There is a man in the minority, and he won't sit in the seat of the scoffers. The righteous man is the man who declines to vote with the majority, when the majority is laughing at the philosophy of goodness.

Now we come to the positive. 'His delight is in the law of Jehovah.' This man is a man who delights in the law of Jehovah, in the fact of it, and in every expression of it. This is the man who believes that the universe is under the mastery of law, that lawlessness in any form is contrary to the highest in the universe. This is the man who says there is delight, and he finds it in the law of Jehovah. He delights in the fact that God is governing and that there is a judgement that discriminates between good and evil. He not only delights in the fact of it, he delights in every expression of it. He knows that every command of God is love-inspired. He knows the truth of what Browning sang: 'I report, as a man may of God's work – all's love, yet all's law.' Law is the outcome of love. There is a man who sings of law, rejoices in law, delights in law.

And then follows another statement about him. He not only delights in it, but 'in His law doth he meditate day and night'. I should not like to take away any value there is in the word 'meditate', but I would like to tell you what it really means. It means 'to talk to himself'. He talks to himself about the law of God. He talks to himself day and night; he soliloquizes. Just as a boy when he is learning his lessons, he learns the law, he repeats the law, he ponders the law. He thinks out loud about it, day and night. There are people who really delight in the law of God as a great principle for the safeguarding of humanity, but who spend little time talking to themselves about it, going over and over it, like a lad conning his lesson until he has got it and it has got him to the end of time. This man will not just make a gesture to the law of God on Sunday morning, once a day on Sunday and then mostly late! Lots of people are doing that – making their gesture to God Almighty and then forgetting about Him and His law for the rest of the week. This man is the man who delights in it and keeps himself in touch with it. He talks to himself about it; he ponders it; it is the secret of his life; he meditates on the law of God day and night.

Then the singer drops into figurative poetry. He tells you what the man is like. He is 'like a tree planted by the streams of water'. 'Planted' – not growing wild! 'Planted by the streams of water, that bringeth forth its fruit in its season' – its own fruit, according to its nature, in its season. 'Whose leaf also doth not wither.' Then he sways back from the figure of the tree to the man. 'And in whatsoever he doeth he shall prosper.'

That is a daring poetic picture. This Hebrew singer takes a tree and makes it the poetic figure of the man he is talking about. The figure is found elsewhere in these psalms. Listen to Psalm 37[5]: 'I have seen the wicked in great power, and spreading himself like a green tree in its native soil.' I purposely went to that psalm, for that describes the wicked – 'spreading himself like a green tree in its native soil'. But notice he was spreading himself like a tree *in his native soil*, not by rivers of water.

What happened to him? The singer goes on: 'But one passed by, and lo, he was not; yea, I sought him, but he could not be found.' He was gone. That is the wicked man, like a tree planted in his own soil.

Then I turn over again, and I find another place where one of these singers is singing – perhaps the same singer, who knows? I am in Psalm 52, and there he says: 'But as for me, I am like a green olive-tree in the house of God. I trust in the loving kindness of God for ever and ever.' He is not planted in his own soil.

I am inclined to go on just once more, and again I find in Psalm $92^{12-13}$ and on: 'The righteous shall flourish like the palm-tree; he shall grow like a cedar in Lebanon. They are planted in the house of Jehovah; they shall flourish in the courts of our God. They shall still bring forth fruit in old age; they shall be full of sap and green; to show that Jehovah is upright.'

Trees, trees, trees! I, too, have seen the wicked spreading himself like a tree in his own soil; but I looked again, and he had vanished! But this man whose delight is in the law of the Lord, who meditates in it day and night, is planted by the streams of water. His life is rooted in the true sources of life. The man who delights in the law of the Lord is the man whose roots run down and find the streams that water and feed him. This man shall bring forth fruit; 'bringeth forth fruit in its season'. Joseph Bryant Rotherham has this interesting and arresting little comment on that. A man who brings forth fruit in his season is the man who, in all the processes of life, brings forth fruit according to purpose; 'that is, learning and liveliness in youth, steady work and sturdy endurance in middle life, patience and serene hope in old age'. That is the fruit of true humanity, rooted in God. A tree planted by the rivers of water: that is the righteous.

Once more. 'Whatsoever he doth shall prosper.' Here the marginal reading is undoubtedly correct. 'He shall prosper in whatsoever he doeth.' That is a much profounder word. It is not always so that what a righteous man does prospers. He fails in it sometimes, but *he* prospers. Joseph was as prosperous in Pharaoh's prison as when he was associated with the throne.

Job was prosperous in the darkness as surely as when he passed into the light. For Joseph the adversity of circumstances passed and the prosperity came, and for Job the outward prosperity came again: but they were both prosperous all the way through.

Quietly now and reverently, Jesus, in whatever He did, prospered. Yet did you ever see any story of any life that, measured by the philosophy of godlessness, was a more ghastly failure? He went from the world with hands and feet pierced with nails, transfixed to a Roman gibbet! Do you call *that* prosperity? Yet, He was prosperous even there, and the pleasure of the Lord prospered in His hands – crucified hands! That is the ultimate word in interpretation of the psalm.

Bring all this to the test of experience. How much there is that seems to contradict it as we look out upon the world today! Is not that so? Does it not seem all through as though wickedness was successful? Oh, yes, and there are psalms that deal with that. Glance at the seventy-third. In the course of it the singer says: 'Behold, these are the wicked; and, being always at ease, they increase in riches. Surely in vain have I cleansed my heart, and washed my hands in innocency; for all the day long have I been plagued, and chastened every morning.' Don't we often feel like that? Well, hear him further: 'If I had said, I will speak thus; behold, I had dealt treacherously with the generation of thy children.' That is how things looked, but he says: 'When I thought how I might know this, it was too painful for me; until I went into the sanctuary of God and considered their latter end.'

It does look as though the wicked were having a good time. There are no pangs in their death; they have an easy time. The righteous are again and again seen battered and bruised with life, until . . . until when? Until they go to the sanctuary of God, the true viewpoint for life. When we get to the sanctuary of God life is seen in its long issues and never measured by the immediate appearances.

It is an old-fashioned view that righteousness pays, but it does. It is an old-fashioned view that wickedness does not, but it never does. The winds of God are blowing, the discriminations of God are active; and, like chaff that the wind drives, the wicked are driven away; all the way of wickedness runs out; there is no goal, no arrival, no destination. But the man who delights in the law of the Lord and meditates in it, his life is like a tree planted by the streams, taking hold of the true sources of life; and he brings forth his fruit and his leaf does not wither; and, in whatsoever he does, he prospers, for he marches through the passing phases of time to the lasting destiny and glory of eternity.

# THE PROOF OF GREATNESS

## Kenneth E. Roach

*And the children of Joseph spake unto Joshua saying, Why hast thou given me but one lot and one portion to inherit, seeing I am a great people, forasmuch as the Lord hath blessed me hitherto? And Joshua answered them, If thou be a great people then get thee to the wood country and cut down for thyself there in the land of the Perizzites and of the giants, if Mount Ephraim be too narrow for thee.*

Joshua 17<sup>14–15</sup>

Joshua 17[14–15]

*Work out your own salvation with fear and trembling, for it is God which worketh in you both to will and to do of his good pleasure.*

Philippians 2[12–13]

This story in the Book of Joshua is an old one, but its message is relevant to every age and generation. The tribe of Joseph had reason to be proud of their fore-father and regarded themselves as an important people, but Joshua had given them just one lot of ground, and they complained: 'Don't you see, we are a great people? Why don't you give us more ground?' Joshua's reply was shrewd and wise. He said in effect: 'There is plenty of land available, but it has to be cleared. If you are a great people, then go up to the hills, cut down the trees, conquer the enemies, claim the land, and prove your greatness by making a place for yourselves, then you will be able to enjoy the fruits of your own labours.'

Whether or not the tribe of Joseph responded to the challenge we do not know: what we do know is that the lesson of this old story has an important message for us today.

*In the first place, it has something to say as to our physical well-being.*

There are people who think that health can be found in a doctor's prescription and that all they have to do is to take the prescribed dose at the correct time. While, however, it is true that medicine does make a major contribution to our health, it is also true that health is the reward of those who discipline themselves in taking exercise and in refraining from excesses; and unless we are prepared to exert ourselves toward physical well-being, the doctor's prescription won't help us very much.

*In the second place, the story has something important to say about our education.*

We are constantly improving our school buildings and installing better equipment. We have excellent textbooks and well-trained teachers; but if the student thinks these facilities will ensure his education, he is in error. The teachers will have to be listened to, the books must be studied, the lessons will have to be learned; but unless the student is prepared to work at the task of learning, there will be no education. There are trees that none but he can cut down; there are problems that he must solve for himself if his mind is to grow; there are enemies of ease and laziness that he must master, and unless he clears the ground for himself he will not possess the rich heritage that is his in our culture. In the last resort, education is something every man must win for himself, or he cannot enjoy it. There are no shortcuts to learning, but to those who bring self-discipline and personal effort the rewards are rich and satisfying.

*A third application of this story may be made to our social life.*

In his Inaugural Address delivered in January 1965, President Lyndon Johnson depicted the 'Great Society'. He painted lovely pictures for the American people. He saw a nation where no one need be poor or illiterate. He showed possibilities of unprecedented affluence and a future that was brighter than anything known before. I believe this dream could still become a reality; but if we Americans think that the 'Great Society' is going to come all 'gift-wrapped' from Washington, we are deluding ourselves. Unfortunately, this is always the temptation in prosperous societies and Welfare States. We learn how to receive and forget how to give; we learn how to play and forget the priority of work; we become accustomed to self-indulgence and forget self-discipline; we expect freedom and good living and forget that it must be deserved and achieved and preserved by untiring diligence and unremitting effort. We had better realize that the 'Great Society' will only come to the extent that we are prepared to work for it, each in his respective sphere; and, if too many Americans fail in this regard, the 'Great Society' will remain only a dream and we shall be doomed to disappointment.

Utopias do not come from welfare offices. If we are a great people, and if we are to realize the 'Great Society', we must work for it with might and main; we must conquer the enemies of hate and fear and prejudice and evil in all its forms; we must get up into the hills and clear the land for ourselves, or there will be no inheritance to enjoy. The price of liberty, as we have been told, is eternal vigilance, and without discipline and self-sacrifice no nation can attain greatness.

President Johnson saw this very plainly. After stating in his Inaugural Address that we have become a nation prosperous, great and mighty, he went on:

But we have no promise from God that our greatness will endure. We have been allowed by Him to see greatness with the sweat of our hands and the strength of our spirit. I do not believe that the Great Society is the ordered, changeless, sterile battalion of the ants: it is the excitement of becoming, always becoming, trying, probing, falling, resting and trying again, but always trying and always gaining. In each generation with tears and toil we have had to earn our heritage again. I will lead as best I can, but look within your own hearts to the old promises and the old dream. They will lead you best of all.

It is to be hoped that every American heard these words, but it is even more important that we do them. It is one thing to have dreams in our hearts: it is another to work for them with our hands. Only as we bend our energies and use our minds for the good of all will the lives of each of us be elated and enriched. We are a great people. Our potential is tremendous. Let us rise to the challenge and prove our greatness in the enemies we conquer and the society we create.

*There is one more application of this ancient story – to the realm of spiritual experience.*

Some of us are praying for a stronger faith and a more virile life. It is right and good for us to pray for such a blessing, but this is yet another ideal for which we must labour. Paul told the Philippians to work out their own salvation with fear and trembling. In Luke's Gospel are recorded the following incisive words of Christ Himself:

Whosoever cometh to Me and heareth My sayings and doeth them, I will show you to whom he is like. He is like a man who built a house and digged deep and laid his foundation on a rock (Luke 6[47–48]).

Jesus is saying here that if the house of our faith is to be strong enough to stand the storms and stresses of life, we must be prepared to dig deep until we find the rock for its foundation. There may be much top-soil to work through; layers of clay will cause difficulty; the rock may be far down: but if we want a faith strong in personal conviction we must dig and keep on digging until we find it.

A vital faith does not come simply by joining a church and supporting its activities. It requires earnest prayer and daily meditation on the Scriptures. It demands reverent worship of God and a striving to be and to do what we see to be His will for our lives. Such a faith will not come easily: it is the fruit of dedicated thought and effort, and has to be worked for. Formal worship must give way to sincere devotion; doubts must be penetrated and personal convictions arrived at; the detached attitude must yield place to the consecrated spirit, and indifference must be replaced by a full commitment to God as He is revealed to us in Jesus Christ. Being a Christian in a general kind of way must be changed to discipleship of the Man of Nazareth. We must set ourselves to learn the great truths He taught; we must be ready to make Him the Lord and Master of our lives; we must follow Him wherever He leads us. If anybody thinks this is easy, it is because he does not know the message of the Gospel or the meaning of true discipleship.

If, however, this sermon were merely an appeal for more self-effort it would not be a fully Christian message. The Bible does not primarily call us to self-discipline: there is something else that makes its tidings Good News. You will notice what Paul adds to the part of the Philippians text which we have just been considering: 'Work out your own salvation with fear and trembling, for it is God which worketh in you both to will and to do of His good pleasure' (Philippians 2$^{12-13}$). The Good News of the Gospel is that we do not work alone in our efforts for righteousness and faith. The resources of the Divine Spirit are working with us and in us toward the same high goals.

Every spring the farmer goes forth to plough and sow his fields, but all his work would produce no harvest without the silent unseen forces at work in nature. The farmer has his work to do, and if he neglects it there will be no crop: but he works in faith because he knows that the material world will back his efforts.

The same is true of the spiritual life. We strive for righteousness and truth and faith, and the Holy Spirit is there to help us. He gives us strength for the weary day, guidance in time of confusion and sustaining grace for every need. Jesus said: 'My Father worketh hitherto, and I work' (John 5¹⁷). This great truth is as real today as it was in the first century. No man is an island; no one stands alone: beside us is the Great Companion; underneath us are the everlasting arms, and within us can be the power of the Eternal Spirit, if we will give Him room in our hearts.

But, like every good father, God does not do for His children what they should and must do for themselves. We must lift up our hearts, straighten our shoulders, tense our muscles, and prepare to work out our own salvation. God stands ready to help those who help themselves, and when we play our part we find the mighty tides of the Holy Spirit ready to guide us toward our high calling in Christ and to strengthen us for the voyage.

My friends: there are hills ahead of us; there is work to be done; there are enemies to be conquered, but we are a great people and, with God beside us, victory is sure and the work itself will prove exhilarating.

Let us rise to the challenge of our time and prove our greatness!

# HOW TO BE SAVED

## WILLIAM EDWIN SANGSTER

*By grace are ye saved through faith.*
Ephesians 2[8]

This was one of the great texts of the Evangelical Revival. Indeed, this is one of the corner-stones of all evangelical truth. It was Martin Luther's mighty watchword. If Spurgeon was suddenly called upon to preach, he found himself most forceful with this theme. Among John Wesley's famous *Forty-Four Sermons* the first is an exposition of this sentence from Paul.

Let me take the text in hand in my own way, as every man must. I propose to examine this grand verse by scrutinizing in turn each of the three keywords. If we can understand what Paul meant by each of these words, and what the evangelical preachers of all ages have meant by them, we shall find that, however the text has been neglected in recent years, this is still the marrow of the Gospel for those of us who believe.

*The word 'grace'*
'By grace are ye saved.'

What do we mean by grace? The old definition called it 'the free, unmerited favour of God'. On that definition I cannot improve. It means that at the heart of all true communion with God there lies this deep

72

truth – that God Himself took the initiative. He loves us better than we can ever love Him. He loves us with a love that does not depend on any answering love of ours. We have not to earn His love, any more than we earned our mother's love. We have but to receive it.

Always the initiative is from God! When you first came to Him, if indeed you *have* come to Him, you came because He first drew you. The very faith by which you lay hold of Him is not of yourself: this also is a gift of God. Nor is it only in the beginning that your salvation is God's free gift. Every onward step you have made in your spiritual pilgrimage has been possible by some bestowing of His grace. Even the life of holiness, to which all the time He is seeking to bring you – the Christlike quality that He wants to repeat in all of His children – even *that* you have not to achieve, but to receive. It is a gift of God.

I know very well that such teaching affronts the modern man, and that many people reject it. The man in the street rejects it tacitly. He may have had nothing to do with religion; but, whenever death is mentioned, he thinks to himself: 'Well, I've never done anyone a bad turn!' In his own mind he believes that, not having been a flagrant sinner, he can work his passage to heaven by the good turns that he has done. I know how our church fathers would have commented on that!

I don't know that any of them ever used this illustration, but I feel sure that something of the sort would have crossed their minds. They would have imagined a man in debt for perhaps half a million pounds, but refusing the help of any friend, and seeking to meet his liabilities by hoarding up his farthings, and coming at last to the audit with elevenpence-halfpenny to set over against a debt of half a million pounds!

There is in man something that rejects the idea of this free and generous forgiving. Of course, it is pride – the deadliest of all the deadly sins. Bernard Shaw may in some things, I suppose, be taken as an example of the modern mind. He says: 'Forgiveness is a beggar's refuge. We must pay our debts.' So speaks the modern man; but, my dear friends, we *cannot* pay our debts. As our spiritual fathers saw so clearly, the only language that we can honestly use in the presence of our awful debt is this prayer:

> *Just as I am, without one plea*
> *But that Thy blood was shed for me,*
> *And that Thou bidd'st me come to Thee,*
>    *O Lamb of God, I come.*

In response to this coming, the free, unmerited favour of God comes to us, cancels the debt, imputes the righteousness of Christ to sinners such as we are; and progessively, as we live with Him, also imparts that righteousness. Here, again, the modern man feels affronted. 'How can the righteousness of anyone else be imputed to me?' asks the critic. 'It is His righteousness, not mine!'

You have heard, perhaps, about the little boy who was dull at school. He was not only dull with his lessons; he also left much to be desired in his conduct. One day he didn't go to school, and his mother said: 'Why aren't you going to school?' He answered: 'We've got a whole holiday. We've won a scholarship.' Notice that he said: '*We've* won a scholarship.' He could have done nothing about it. A lad as dull as he would have been incapable of winning a scholarship. In the school a clever boy who concentrated had achieved that distinction. And yet, without hesitation – and no doubt with gratitude! – the dull little lad reported: 'We've won a scholarship!'

This is only a simple example, but I think it will help you to understand a little of what we mean by imputing righteousness. God permits the purity of Jesus to cover us. The hymn writer puts it like this:

> *Jesu, Thy blood and righteousness*
> *My beauty are, my glorious dress;*
> *Midst flaming worlds, in these arrayed,*
> *With joy shall I lift up my head.*

No wonder, then, that in all the rapture of a fine hymn Samuel Davies cries out:

> *In wonder lost, with trembling joy*
> *We take the pardon of our God.*

And Charles Wesley sings:

> *Amazing love! How can it be*
> *That Thou, my God, shouldst die for me?*

In addition to the imputing of righteousness, God likewise imparts it. When any penitent sinner first comes to Him, God imputes His righteousness. Then, as we live with Him, He also imparts righteousness, progressively. It is a part of the Holy Spirit's work to make us holy, too. He sets out not only to justify us, but to sanctify us, and all the time the whole work is by grace. *Grace!* The free, unmerited favour of God! The grace that today is flowing like a river! The grace to which any needy person may turn with eagerness now!

### The word 'saved'

'By grace are ye saved.'

Whenever we use the word 'saved' some people at once think of hell or heaven. Being saved means to them just that – escaping hell, achieving heaven. But that is a very limited way to think of this term 'saved'. For instance, it puts the whole matter in the future. Now, we are on earth, not in heaven, and we can be saved now. The Scripture says: 'He that believeth on the Son hath eternal life.' He has it here and now!

Salvation is not from earth, but from sin. It is deliverance not merely from the penalty of sin, but also from the fact of sin. Those of you who are theologically-minded may be thinking that I am confusing salvation and sanctification. Still I say that the outworking of salvation gives us deliverance from the sins of the flesh and likewise from the sins of the mind.

Think of the men who have been hopelessly imprisoned by thirst for strong drink, and yet have been delivered from that bondage. Think of the men who have been eaten up with lust – whose heads, in the words of Montaigne, have been 'merry-go-rounds of lustful images'. Think of people in the grip of greed, who become as metallic as the coins they seek. All of these are victims of present sins, and from these present sins there is for each of them a present salvation.

Not only from the sins of the flesh! There is likewise deliverance from the sins of the mind. From jealousy,

and all the canker that it brings; from gossip, and all the
evil that it entails; from pride, the most subtle of sins.
From all of these there is salvation, here and now.

Don't, then, think of salvation solely in terms of
heaven. Think also in terms of a higher quality of life
here on earth. In the light of Christ examine your own
heart, and you may find yourself praying like this: 'O
God, I am selfish. Too often other folk come second or
third in my thoughts. In myself I have discovered
jealousy. In the face of some temptations I am terribly
weak. I cannot forgive people; I do not truly and deeply
forgive. If they speak to me unkindly, hot burning
words rush to my lips, and I want to sting them back. O
God, it is hell to live this way at its worst. It must be
heaven to be like Christ. If He can get me out of all
this, and impart to me His quality of life, then I am
saved, and He is My Saviour.'

Have you this quality of life? When you think of
Jesus, does the hunger for such a way of living come to
you? Do you yearn to be like Him? This is what is in
my mind when I think of your being saved. Once again,
I remind you of this simple truth: 'By grace are ye
saved.'

### The word 'faith'

'By grace are ye saved through faith.'

Like the word 'grace' and the word 'saved', the term
'faith', is often misunderstood. Many people agree with
the statement of the schoolboy: 'Faith is believing
what you know to be untrue!' Even more elderly and
serious commentators regard faith as primarily a matter
of the mind.

There are many definitions of faith. No definition

can be satisfactory if it confines faith merely to belief. That would make it merely the mental acknowledgement of some external fact, and would not include at its very heart the spirit of trust. This is the keyword of faith: it means to 'trust'. Faith is not merely an expression of belief. It is a venture of the whole personality in trusting one who is worthy.

Nor is it right to think, as some people do, that faith belongs only to religion. All life is by faith. When you board a bus you have faith – faith that the driver knows his job. When you go to a restaurant for a meal, you have faith – faith that the food is wholesome and well-cooked. When you send your child to school you have faith – faith that the teacher will not poison his mind.

Even science proceeds largely on faith. Contrary to the opinions of some people who haven't thought the matter through, no one can prove the great principles on which scientists proceed, such principles as the uniformity of nature and the conservation of energy. But, in order to proceed at all, scientists must assume such basic principles. All business, too, is built on credit. The word 'credit' is simply the Latin form of 'trust'.

If, then, we find faith everywhere else, should it surprise us to find it also in religion? In common life and in school, in science and in business, we find faith everywhere. But only in religion do we find it supremely. Just as in the scale of values nothing about a man is so precious as his soul, so the faith through which that soul can be saved must ever be the supreme expression of human trust.

Let me ask: Are you conscious of your own need? At the same time, are you aware of your weakness, of the pressure of your sins, of the dark problems in your life and of your inability alone to grapple with them? Do you feel that you need the help of someone else? It is to such needs that the Gospel speaks about your being saved.

If you have never yet ventured on Christ, I plead with you to do so now. If you have already received a timorous faith, I urge you to venture on Him far more completely, to recognize that the real end of faith is to unite the person who believes with the Person on whom he believes, and that only as you are united with Christ through faith can you have the quality of life which is the sterling of eternity.

This is the glad Good News that the evangelists carried everywhere in the first century and that their true followers have echoed in every century since. Our Wesleyan fathers sounded it with tremendous power in the eighteenth century. In an age when most people had lost all hope, when they mistakenly thought that God was not there, or that He was not kind, the spokesmen for God came with the burning message that He *was* there and that He *was* kind; that by His free generosity men could be lifted into fullness of life, if only they trusted in Christ. This is still the heart of the Gospel. I sound it again, and with jubilation.

Nineteen hundred years after the apostles first proclaimed this Gospel, and more than two hundred years after John Wesley first received it in his heart, I again offer you this Gospel: 'By grace are ye saved through faith.'

# SIN AND FORGIVENESS

## Alexander Ross

*I have blotted out, as a thick cloud, thy transgressions,
and, as a cloud, thy sins: return unto Me, for I have
redeemed thee.*                                      Isaiah 44²²

In his *Grace Abounding* John Bunyan tells us about
the time when he tried to run away from God, like him
who said:

> *I fled Him, down the nights and down the days;*
> *I fled Him, down the arches of the years;*
> *I fled Him, down the labyrinthine ways*
> *Of my own mind; and in the mist of tears*
> *I hid from Him, and under running laughter. . . .*
> *From those strong Feet that followed, followed after.*

In those 'flying fits', as he describes them, Bunyan says
that this Scripture would call, as running after him:
'I have blotted out, as a thick cloud, thy transgressions,
and as a cloud thy sins: return unto Me, for I have
redeemed thee.' 'This,' he says, 'would make me a little
stop and, as it were, look over my shoulder behind me,
to see if I could discern that the God of grace would
follow me with a pardon in His hand.' What a difference
it would make if all who sit listening to the Gospel had a
vision like that given to them!

It is surely the Sufferer of Isaiah 53 who speaks here. The Sufferer who has made Atonement once for all for human sin. It is God in Christ who declares here, in memorable words, that since full Atonement has been made for sin, He is now waiting to be gracious, for 'His love unknown has broken every barrier down' that sin has erected between us and Him.

*Think of the view of sin suggested here.*

There is nothing that the modern world needs so much as a new vision of God in His holiness and His abhorrence of sin. Such a vision would lead inevitably, as in the case of Isaiah of old, to another vision which should slay our spiritual pride for ever – the vision of sin in its horror, its filthiness and its guiltiness. Dr Andrew Bonar once said: 'It is a real sense of sin that in a moment explains to us the richest figures in the Bible.'

We have a deeply-instructive figure here. What is the conception of sin that is hinted at in the expression 'blotted out'? In Isaiah 43²⁵ God says: 'I, even I, am He that blotteth out thy sins'; and in the opening words of the fifty-first Psalm David prays: 'According to the multitude of Thy tender mercies, blot out my trans-gressions.'

In these passages the idea suggested seems to be that of a black record which stands against us in God's Book, a record which gets blacker and blacker, and more and more damning, so long as we refuse to seek His for-giveness. 'Could my tears for ever flow', however sincere they might be as an expression of sorrow over sin, there is not potency enough in them to wash out one line, or one word, of the terrible record.

But, serious as that way of looking at sin undoubtedly

is, it would appear that a still more serious view of it is suggested here. This verse leads us out into a larger universe, for it surely means that sin is something that has darkened the whole universe and has caused black thunderclouds to roll between us and the Holy One, from whom, as Isaiah says in a later passage, our sins have separated us, by hiding His face from us.

When we think of our plight in this way, it is not the outward and superficial aspect of our lives that troubles us. We thoroughly agree now with the standpoint of the man who said:

> *It is not what my hands have done*
> *That weighs my spirit down,*
> *That brings a darkness o'er the sun*
> *And over earth a frown.*

Casual observers of his life, he says, may see little wrong in it. But he surveys himself from the inside and feels mournfully:

> *How deep the principle of sin*
> *Its roots may there conceal within,*
> *And spread its poison through the frame*
> *Without a deed that man may blame!*

We need the light of the Great White Throne to shine, not only on the outside of our lives but into all the dark corners of our hearts, and then we shall realize that 'naked to His glance our secret sins' are in the light of the pure countenance of Him with whom we have to do. John Keble prayed that no 'earth-born cloud' might ever hide God from his eyes. The clouds are earth-born,

born in the corrupt heart of man and darkening the universe.

This verse speaks of a 'cloud' and it speaks of a 'thick cloud'. Some clouds are fleecy wisps of moisture; others are thunderclouds of inky blackness: but the white fleecy clouds as well as the dark clouds can hide the sun from us. There are some foul sins which seem to cry loudly to high heaven for judgement and punishment, and there are other sins which men may be inclined to think of as little sins, sins not worth bothering about. But the little sins may hide the face of God from us; and, as Paul says, 'The wrath of God is revealed from heaven against all ungodliness and unrighteousness of men, who hold down the truth in unrighteousness' (Romans 1$^{18}$,R.V.), or, as Bishop Moule of Durham paraphrased the apostle's meaning, 'who suppress the truth, living in unrighteousness the while.'

*Think of the radiant description of the forgiveness of sins that is given here.*

In his rich volume of sermons, *The Way Everlasting* – a book which it is not easy to lay hands on nowadays – Dr James Denney suggests that there are three ways in which we can think of the forgiveness of sins. We may say that it is impossible. Things are what they are and the consequences of them will be what they will be, and they cannot be reversed. No one who really knows the message which the Bible brings to us can rest long in the creed of blank pessimism. Another thing that may be said is that forgiveness may be taken for granted because God is so loving and merciful that no sinner will be left unforgiven throughout eternity. That may be a far more dangerous way of looking at things than the first way, for it seems to involve a shallow and trivial conception of sin in its deserts and its consequences. There is a third way, the biblical way. 'Forgiveness,' as Denney puts it, 'is not impossible, nor is it a matter of course. As the New Testament holds it out to sinful men, it is the supreme achievement of God in Christ – His costliest, His unspeakable gift.'

A statement like that is in perfect harmony with what the one hundred and thirtieth Psalm says about forgiveness: 'If Thou wert to mark iniquity, O Lord, who shall stand?' These are the words of a man who is very far indeed from taking forgiveness for granted, yet who can go on to say: 'But' – and can we not hear the note of triumph in his voice? – 'there is forgiveness with Thee', with the miracle-working God alone, with Him who says: 'I, even I, and I alone, am He that blotteth out. . .'

Some people are strongly blind to the fact that there is in the Old Testament a great Gospel for sinners, a Gospel which is set forth with quite a variety of figurative language. We are told that God casts our sins into the deep places of the sea, that He casts them behind His back and that He puts them as far from us as the east is distant from the west. But is there any figure that is so rich in meaning as the one here brought before us?

No human hand can reach up to scatter the clouds which may oppress our spirits; clouds, I mean, in the realm of nature. Only God can do that when He makes His sun to shine on us again. We look up at one moment and the sky is completely overcast. We look up some time afterwards when the sun has broken through the clouds, and not one speck of cloud can now be seen, only that dome of blue from horizon to horizon, while the glorious sun lights up the world. That is a truly radiant image; and, like the other Old Testament figures that have been mentioned, it sets forth the completeness of God's pardon. 'He pardons with overflowing love.'

If we desire to get some light on the mystery of forgiveness, if we desire to know how it is possible for the holy God to forgive sins, we must visit Calvary. We have already noted the words of God in Isaiah 43[25]. Notice now the words of the preceding verse, where God says: 'Thou hast made Me to serve with thy sins, thou hast wearied Me with thine iniquities.' As Delitzsch says in his Commentary on Isaiah, God declares in that verse that 'the sins of Israel pressed upon Him as a burden does upon a servant. His love took upon itself the burden of Israel's guilt, which derived its gravitating force from His own holy righteous wrath; but it was a severe task to bear this heavy burden, and expunge it – a thoroughly divine task, the significance of which was first brought out in its own true light by the Cross on Golgotha.'

On the day of the Crucifixion the holy soul of Jesus entered into a more awful darkness than the supernatural darkness which covered the land of Palestine for three hours. In that darkness He endured to the uttermost limit the penalty demanded by the broken law of God, and from the heart of His 'unknown sufferings' He cried: 'My God, My God, why hast Thou forsaken Me?' The Scottish poetess, Mrs Cousin, who wrote 'The Sands of Time are Sinking', and who has been described as 'a Scottish Christina Rossetti, with a more pronounced theology', wrote a richly theological poem on the Atonement, which contains this verse:

> *The Holy One did hide His face;*
> *O Christ, 'twas hid from Thee!*
> *Dumb darkness wrapt Thy soul a space,*
> *The darkness due to me;*
> *But now that face of radiant grace*
> *Shines out in love on me.*

Words and thoughts like these make us bow our heads in worship when we visit Calvary and ought to move us to say, with Bunyan's Pilgrim, 'He hath given me rest by His sorrow and life by His death'; yes, we may go on to say: 'Because He stood condemned in my room and stead, He has won for me the shining of the eternal love on my soul, which had dwelt so long in the dark.'

Dr F. W. Boreham in one of his books has an interesting reference to our text. He narrates how he was sitting one day on a lovely and extensive lawn, when a gloomy hush seemed to have settled down on everything. But, an hour later, the wind changed, a cool breeze swept across the lawn and through a rift in the clouds the sun peered forth. At once, he says, he became aware of the chirping of insects in the grass; a thrush began to pour out its gladdest notes from a giant elm; a blackbird in a fir tree answered it. As soon as the clouds were lifted, the singing began. Of course! What does the prophet go on to say here? 'Sing, O ye heavens; for the Lord hath done it: shout, ye lower parts of the earth: break forth into singing, ye mountains, O forest, and every tree therein: for the Lord hath redeemed Jacob, and glorified Himself in Israel.'

The redeemed man, as Wade Robinson says, enters into a new world of light and peace, with bluer heavens above him and a greener earth around him, and the birds singing gladder songs on every bush and tree.

Have we really entered into that new world? Has the singing really begun?

# THE POWER OF HIS RESURRECTION

## James S. Stewart

*Now the God of peace, that brought again from the dead our Lord Jesus, that great Shepherd of the sheep, through the blood of the everlasting covenant, make you perfect in every good work to do His will, working in you that which is well pleasing in His sight, through Jesus Christ; to Whom be glory for ever and ever. Amen.*

Hebrews 13[20-21]

The most characteristic word of the Christian religion is the word Resurrection. If you had to choose one word to gather up and focus and express the very essence of the faith, would this not have to be your choice?

For this is what Christianity essentially is – a religion of Resurrection. This is what every worshipping congregation is intended in the purpose of God to be – a community of the Resurrection. And this is what the Gospel offers today to this dark and ruined world, where men peering into the future are daunted by the wellnigh impossible task of creating order out of chaos and life out of death – the power of the Resurrection. In short, this is the essential Gospel. Rejoice that the Lord is arisen!

It is true, of course, that for us Christians the Cross must ever stand at the very heart of things. If we bungling, sinful creatures lose sight of the Cross even

88

for a day, we are done for – and we know it. But a man may gaze at the Cross and miss the Gospel that saves – for he is still on the wrong side of Easter. This is Christianity's symbol – not the dead figure of the crucifix, but Christ risen, trampling a broken Cross beneath His feet! 'Neither is there salvation in any other.'

Far too often we have regarded the Resurrection as an epilogue to the Gospel, an addendum to the scheme of salvation, a codicil to the divine last will and testament – thereby falsifying disastrously the whole emphasis of the Bible. The fact is there would never have been a New Testament at all, apart from the burning certainty of all its writers that He whose mighty deeds they were recording had conquered death and was alive for ever. This was no mere appendix to the faith: this was, this is, the faith – the overpowering, magnificent good news. Rejoice that the Lord is arisen!

There is no darkness which this does not illuminate, no despair this does not smite with sudden hope.

Test it and see.

For example, many in these tense, tumultuous days are trembling for the ark of God, haunted by the fear that the powers of darkness may ultimately defeat the dreams for which Christ died. Many are paralysed by that terrible doubt. But Easter means that God has already taken the measure of the evil forces at their very worst and most malignant, that He has met the challenge precisely at that point and routed the darkness and settled the issue. Rejoice that the Lord is arisen!

Or the trouble may be more personal. Many are feeling strained and depressed and tired out, and quite inadequate for life, worried by the failure and the muddle of their own experience. But Easter means a living, radiant Christ walking at your side on the weariest Emmaus Road. Rejoice that the Lord is arisen!

Or the burden of the mystery may be heavier still. It may be that someone whom you loved the best has left you and passed out of sight for ever across the river, journeying away to the country from whose bourne no traveller returns. But Easter means One has returned, to tell you of the glory yonder. Rejoice that the Lord is arisen!

Test it and see. Here is an evangel to scatter every darkness and to exhilarate every broken spirit with strength and courage. This is the only Gospel the New Testament knows. He is risen indeed. O magnify the Lord with me!

Let us take one of the most moving and memorable expressions of the Easter truth ever penned. In Hebrews 13²⁰⁻²¹ we read: 'Now the God of peace, that brought again from the dead the Lord Jesus, that great Shepherd of the sheep, through the blood of the everlasting covenant, make you perfect in every good work to do His will, working in you that which is well pleasing in His sight, through Jesus Christ; to Whom be glory for ever and ever.'

*The mighty act of God*

Notice particularly how the writer puts it. He says, speaking of the Resurrection – 'It was God who did this thing. It was God's mighty act that brought up the Lord Jesus from the dead.'

This emphasis is characteristic of all the men of the New Testament. It is immensely significant that these first Christians never preached the Resurrection simply as Jesus' escape from the grave, as the reanimation of One who had died, or as the return of the Master to His friends. They always proclaimed it as the living God in omnipotent action. It was God's hands that had taken the stone which the builders rejected, and made it the head of the corner. 'This is the Lord's doing,' they declared, 'and it is marvellous in our eyes.'

Their insight taught them that it was what lay behind the Resurrection that mattered. And what lies behind it is this – God vindicating the dreams for which Christ died; God ratifying righteousness, justice, and truth against the evil powers that hate these things and seek to crush and crucify them; God announcing His invincible divine determination to make Christ Lord of all.

It is at this point that the Resurrection fact strikes right into world history as it confronts us today. This is the dramatic relevance of Easter to our own confused, bewildered age. For if the power that was strong enough to get Jesus out of the grave, mighty enough to shatter and confound the whole hideous demonic alliance of evil, creative enough to smite death with resurrection – if this power is in action still (as the basic proclamation of Christianity declares), why then, you and I can lift up our heads, knowing and rejoicing that 'God is on the field when He is most invisible.' He shall not fail nor be discouraged till He has established truth for ever in the earth, and brought in the kingdom of heaven.

*The available power*

But the message comes home to us more intimately than this. For see how this writer to the Hebrews continues: 'Now may God, who brought again from the dead the Lord Jesus, make you perfect in every good

work to do His will, working in you that which is well
pleasing in His sight.' That is to say, the same divine
creative energy which resurrected Christ is available
for you, for me: and that, mark you, not only at death
to raise us up, but here and now to help us to live.

Who could realize this and not be thrilled by it?
Here is the apostle praying for those Christians and for
that Church, that the identical force which God had
exerted in taking Jesus out of the grave might operate
on a similar scale in their own lives, might go inwardly
to work to make them strong and pure and brave and
vital – to make them, in short, resurrected personalities,
throbbing with new life!

I sometimes wonder if we have ever really compre-
hended that this – nothing less – is what the Gospel
offers: the power which shattered death for Jesus, to
help us now to live!

It is surely worth our pondering. Here was the Lord
Christ, wounded and burdened and bowed down with
human sin, cut off from the land of the living, with
everything apparently lost, and all His hopes and dreams
(so the world thought) dead and done for and defeated –
and God by one mighty act of power, by the sheer
energy of grace, had brought Him through and set
Him on high: and now for ever that same power – not
something different, but that identical energy – available
for you, for me, for all who will receive it!

Too often we are like the man with the rake in
Bunyan's dream, gazing permanently downwards, ob-
sessed with such poor sticks and straws and dust as our
own weak efforts of will, our own ineffectual resolves
and insubstantial, wistful longings: never dreaming
that the Lord God who resurrected Christ is standing

there beside us, with that gift of supernatural power – ours, if we would have it!

It is this which explains the irrepressible excitement of early Christianity. They went, those followers of Jesus, to men who had been morally and spiritually defeated scores, hundreds, of times and they said: 'Here is a way of victory! God has brought again from the dead the Lord Jesus. With such a power at work, what may happen – for you?'

That was the message. And lest any of their hearers should think they were being merely rhetorical and romantic, always those men of the New Testament went on to say: 'We know it, for we have proved it. It has worked for us!'

The truth of that claim is apparent. How was it that a little group of men in an upper room – ordinary, fallible, blundering men – were able to go out and turn the world upside down? It was not that they were commanding personalities – most of them were not. It was not that they had official backing, impressive credentials, or illustrious patronage: of all that they had less than nothing. It was this – that they had established contact with the power that had resurrected Jesus; or, rather, that this unearthly power had laid hold upon them.

And still today they accost us, saying: 'It is abroad now in the earth, the power of the Resurrection. Why not for you?' And they look at us with absolute assurance: 'Why not for you?'

But we are so slow to take it in. We are like our forefathers who lived all their days in a world containing the marvel of electricity, and never guessed that it was there! Dr Johnson once said a striking thing about Oliver Goldsmith: 'He would be a great man, if he realized the wealth of his internal resources.' If only we Christians would come awake to that!

But we hesitate. 'It can't apply to us,' we say. 'Our lives are not the stuff out of which God's Easter victories are made. And as for hoping to live on Christ's level, with that new, risen quality of life, why, what's the use? All very well to talk like that, but we stopped trying long ago. It can't be for us – our problems are too many, our thwarting frailties too baffling, our chains of defeat too firmly shackled on our souls. We have toiled all night and taken nothing.' And so we go on our way with what Thomas Carlyle noted in Coleridge: 'a look of anxious impotence in his eyes'.

But these men of the New Testament will not accept that denial. 'You surely don't imagine,' they cry to us, 'that the power which took Christ out of the grave is going to be baffled by you? That the God who did that terrific thing is going to find your little problem too hard for Him to deal with? That the God who, in the mighty act of Easter broke through the last darkness of the universe, is going to confess Himself impotent on the scale of your little life, and say: "No, I cannot work any miracles here: this is too intractable for Me"? But that does not make sense,' those writers say, 'that doubt is utterly irrational! He that brought again from the dead the Lord Jesus, shall He not – today if you will ask Him – revive and quicken you?'

*The way of self-commitment*

This, however, must be added: there is one condition. Before the creative God can come into our life, before this dynamic reality can lay hold of us, before our spirits can know the baptism of power and of eternity, one thing is needful. Self-surrender! Self-commitment!

And this writer to the Hebrews has very dramatically reminded us of that. For did you notice that even this magnificent triumphant verse has a streak of blood across it? Did you hear, through this shout of Easter praise and the trumpets of victory, the diapason note of sacrifice? 'The God of peace brought again from the dead the Lord Jesus, through the blood of the everlasting covenant.' There was no road to Easter for Jesus except by Good Friday; no way to that risen, eternal quality of life except by life laid down. And, that being so, this, too, is axiomatic – there is no road to the power of Easter for any of us except at the cost of self-commitment; no way to the experience of having God's energies loosed and set free into our life except through the discipline of self-surrender. That is the condition.

Here, then, is the question each of us must face. With this supernatural force waiting to be used, this power that resurrected Christ and energized the Church and made life new for multitudes – with this available, why should my life ever be helpless and maimed and impoverished and defeated? Is it that I have been unwilling to travel the road that Jesus went and all the saints – the exacting road of consecration?

The ultimate secret of Resurrection power was given by William Cowper in the lines we often sing:

> *The dearest idol I have known,*
> *Whate'er that idol be,*
> *Help me to tear it from Thy throne,*
> *And worship only Thee.*

That is the streak of blood. That is the Good Friday sacrifice. And beyond it – all the power of Easter, all the efficiency of a conquering soul, all the thrill of being risen with Christ, all the marvel of life blossoming red from the dust of self's defeat.

# HIS GREATEST HOUR

## D. P. Thomson

*In the year that King Uzziah died I saw the Lord.*
Isaiah 6[1]

That was the greatest hour of Isaiah's life – greater than any that had gone before, greater than any that was to come after.

It was the hour when the world of unseen realities broke through for the first time on his consciousness; when what he had taken for granted as background became a living, glowing reality right in the foreground of his experience. It was the hour when he lay in the dust of the temple floor; the hour when he saw himself with a clarity that brought to focal point on his lips the festering sores of his own inner life.

It was the hour when the cleansing fires of heaven, searing the lips that had been stained with evil, swept right through the very fibres of his being; the hour of his complete and utter commitment, from which he rose to his feet a wholly dedicated man.

And this may be the great hour of your life – greater than any that has gone before, greater than any that will come after. If I didn't believe that, I wouldn't be standing here today. If that were not so, then this service in which you and I are engaged would be a sheer irrelevance and a mockery. For God is here, and Christ is here and the Holy Ghost is here – and you are here: in all your need and helplessness, in all your self-complacency and blindness, and with all your unrealized possibilities of better and bigger and finer things than you have ever been or done!

Make no mistake about it: the greatest hour in a man's life is not the hour in which he realizes the ambition on which for years he has set his heart. It is not the hour when he stands crowned at last, amid the plaudits of the multitude, with the laurels for which he has toiled so hard. It is not the hour when he looks with the eyes of love and hope and longing, of utter trust and complete self-giving, into the face of the woman with whose life his own is even then being linked in the closest and most enduring of all human ties. It is the hour when he meets with God, the hour that changes everything.

It is the hour when the vision of things unseen breaks for the first time on his soul; the hour when the wonder and the majesty of God humble him, as it were, to the very dust; the hour when his own involvement in the shame and tragedy of the world's sin becomes a piercing reality to him; the hour when the tides of the Spirit sweep through his very being, cleansing at once the dirt and the dross; the hour when all that he is, all that he has and all that he ever may be, is laid down in glad and grateful surrender at his Master's feet. And that hour may come for you this morning, here in this church, in this very service, before we sing our closing hymn or while we are singing it.

We are not told how old Isaiah was. There is something deeply significant about all the silences of Scripture. It is as though the writer is saying to us: 'It can happen to

you while you are still young. It can come to you
in the middle time of the years. It can bring you
right into the scope of God's great purpose for men
long after the shadows of evening have begun to
gather.'

That is one of the great lessons we have been learning
these past months in the work in which I am privileged
to be engaged. I have seen men and women changed in
their teens and early twenties; I have seen them transformed in their thirties, forties, and fifties; and I have
seen them brought to a first vital experience of the
reality and presence and power of the living God – and
so altered in the whole form and texture of their life
and outlook that their wives could hardly believe that
they were the same men they had married – when they
were in their sixties and seventies.

I know now that there is no limit to what the power
of God can do, and I want to say to you here, today,
that He can do it now, for you.

What was it that happened to Isaiah in that hour?

*This, first, that he became aware of God in a completely
new way.*

There was a very real sense in which he had always
believed in Him, always known about Him, always
trusted Him, always acknowledged the fact of His
presence and activity – in mercy as well as in judgement
– in history, in biography and in experience.

It could hardly have been otherwise with a man
brought up in a land and among a people such as his.
But in no true sense had God ever become real to him
before, right there in the foreground of his consciousness at the point of his own deep need, utterly relevant

to the situation in which he found himself at that hour, and in complete command of that situation. For if there was an empty throne that day in Israel there was, still more obviously, and much more painfully and meaningfully, an empty throne in Isaiah's own heart! And, remember this, there may be niches in our hearts for many, but there is a throne only for God!

Is that not what you and I need today? – to become aware of God in a sense in which we have never done before; to realize His utter relevancy to the situation that confronts us in the tortured, fearful world outside, and in the tormenting world of conflicting passions, of contending hopes and fears in our own heart and life; to know, beyond all shadow of doubt, that He is indeed in control, and to make sure that so far as we ourselves are concerned the control of our lives has passed into His hands?

*What was it that happened to Isaiah? He saw himself in a wholly new light.*

He realized for the first time that he was a sinner, stained with the prevailing impurity of his people, as much a participant in their guilt as he had been a sharer of their fellowship. Utterly broken, he lay there, at once soiled and contaminated by the world in which he lived and worked, and from whose atmosphere and outlook, whose forms of thought and speech, whose standards of value and modes of action it was so impossible for him to escape.

Is that not true of us? Is it not true of you, because of where you have to live and what you can't escape seeing, because of where you have to work and what you can't help hearing? There are places to which you must go; there are things you must do; there are people with whom you must mix. And some of the dirt sticks. For worse as well as better, you are involved in your environment.

But there is a much bigger problem than that! Isaiah found himself part of the corporate iniquity of his people – a target for the righteous wrath of God because of what they had failed to do, as well as for what they had done amiss.

Today, in a world of horrible and hideous injustice, of mounting and crushing armaments, of haunting and terrifying fears, of scores of millions of homeless or half-starving people, of lost moorings and vanished hopes and disappearing moral standards, there is no escape for you or for me – in so far as we have done nothing or done too little about it – have failed even to raise our voices in protest against it – we stand condemned in the final court of all. And in the clear pure light of God's presence we can only say: 'Undone!'

*What was it that finally happened to Isaiah? He passed through a spiritual experience so transforming that it involved both cleansing and commitment.*

In the hour of a man's deepest need it is not the vision of new horizons for which his soul cries out. It is for a new and nobler ideal of life-service that he yearns with all the intensity of his being. It is not for a new and more wonderful fellowship, or for a more powerful dynamic. It is for the cleansing power of the living God to sweep right down to the depths of his nature, for his mind and heart and will – the inner springs of motive and desire and action – to be purged and purified as they have never been before, whatever the humiliation, the pain or the cost may be.

And it was just that that Isaiah got – and that you can get, in this very hour and place, just right where you are sitting, in your pew in church this morning.

> *Just as I am without one plea,*
> *But that Thy blood was shed for me,*
> *And that Thou bidd'st me come to Thee,*
> *O, Lamb of God, I come.*

And for Isaiah it meant committal – complete, final, irrevocable – the giving of himself to God without any reservation whatever. Have you given yourself yet to the God who wants you and needs you, who has for you a place in His heart of love and in His plan of life, who alone can make you what in your heart of hearts you want to be, who is ready to take you now, just as you are, and with what you have to bring?

> *Take my life, and let it be*
> *Consecrated, Lord, to Thee.*
> *Take my will, it is Thine own;*
> *It shall be Thy royal throne.*
> *Take myself, and I will be*
> *Ever, only, all for Thee!*

# 'I HAVE KEPT THE FAITH'

## JAMES KYD THOMSON

*I have kept the faith.*        2 Timothy 4[7]

*It was about the only thing Paul* had *kept.*

Other things he had thrown away or they had been taken from him. He had thrown away much that every Jew in those days prized. In his letter to his Philippian friends he refers to that. 'Whoever thinks he can rely on outward privilege', he writes to them, 'I can outdo him. I was circumcised on the eighth day after birth. I belonged to the race of Israel, to the tribe of Benjamin. I was the Hebrew son of Hebrew parents, a Pharisee as regards the law, in point of ardour a persecutor of the Church, immaculate by the standard of legal righteousness.'

Paul's thoughts are running back there to the time before his conversion when he was a young man. The ball was at his feet then. He had not only a brilliant mind and a fervent heart to sweep him on to a dazzling career; he had many extrinsic advantages, advantages of birth and social position and training, and not unlikely the advantage of plentiful means. But all these advantages he had thrown away. 'They seemed gains to me then,' he writes. 'I gloried in them, prided myself on them, enjoyed them; but after I came to know Jesus Christ, I threw them all away. In comparison with

Him, they did not seem to me worth the keeping.'

And there were other things most men prize that had been denied to Paul, or that had been taken from him.

For example, his health was precarious; he was subject to the attacks of a painful disease. He had no home of his own to be a rest to his heart, no wife to cheer him, no kindred who would own him. For daily bread he had been dependent on the laborious work of his own hands and the occasional kindness of others. He had nothing laid by. Some staunch friends he had kept, but others had deserted him, and even turned against him.

'The first time I had to defend myself,' he says in this letter to Timothy, 'I had no supporters. Every one deserted me.'

Can you see Paul, then, writing this letter – an old man, sitting chained in jail, with death only round the corner, desperately poor, feeble in health, friendless, and alone?

Almost the only thing he had kept was the faith that Jesus had given him.

*But, to Paul, that was the one thing most worth keeping.*

Everything else he was content to lose so long as he kept that. Health, wealth, home and friends, freedom, the glittering prizes of life – he could be content without them all, content and satisfied so long as he kept his faith. To him that was the one thing needful, worth more than anything else.

For what is it that we seek in any possession? Is it not some satisfaction? Is it not satisfaction that we are all seeking?

Well, Paul found in his faith abounding and permanent satisfaction, the satisfaction of his whole nature.

It satisfied his mind. Thinker as he was – and his was one of the great intellects of the world – he could never be at ease until he had found some philosophy of the universe in which his mind could rest. Men like him are haunted by the ultimate questions: Whence have we come? Whither do we go? Why are we here? Is there any purpose in the world? Any meaning in human life?

To questions like these Paul found in his faith an answer in which his mind could rest. It did not clear up every mystery for him. But his faith did at least make sense of the world to Paul. It gave a clue for the unravelling of mysteries. It assured him that there was a gracious meaning, a wonderful and glorious purpose in what would otherwise have been a senseless, bitter, heart-breaking, unredeemed tragedy of a world.

If his faith satisfied his mind, it did more than satisfy his conscience. It cleansed it. How sharp-toothed his conscience was we can see for ourselves in the seventh chapter of Romans. All the wretchedness of the bad conscience was known to Paul until, taking his stand by the Cross of Christ, he could look his sins in the face and find rest from them and peace.

Further, Paul was that rare combination – a great thinker who is also a great man of action. Life could never have been worthwhile for such as he unless he had found something greatly worthwhile to do, toil at and live for, not some little thing that might grow under his hands but pass and die when he did, but some big enduring thing that would draw out all there was in him.

In his fight for the faith he found the most satisfying

of all possible expressions for the fiery energy of his soul. Life could never be dull, idle, trivial for Paul when there was Christ to live and work and die for.

And not mind and conscience and will alone were satisfied by his faith. Paul had a big, human, deeply affectionate heart that craved for friendship, that felt loneliness as a burden, that knew the need of comfort and sustaining. And when he could find all that nowhere else, he found it to the full in his faith.

It is satisfaction men seek. Paul had found it, full and lasting, the satisfaction of not just one little bit of himself, which is all men commonly find, but of his whole nature, and the roots of it were in his faith.

That was the only thing he had kept; but it was the biggest and the best of all his possessions, the one most worth keeping.

*At times he did not find it easy to keep.*

There was so much within himself that menaced it, so much without that seemed to laugh at it as preposterous.

And here, at least, you and I have kinship with Paul. I don't know that you and I could be content though all else were taken away, if only faith were left. I don't know that faith seems to us as it seemed to him, the most priceless of all possessions. But, we come near to him at this point, that faith is not easy. It has never been easy all the time for anyone. There is no backbone in the faith that is easy.

To begin with, of course, we believed what we were told. We took our faith at second-hand from others. And then, in our teens, perhaps, the questioning and the struggle began. We read books; we met people who scoffed at the Christian faith. And some of these books impressed us by their mental power, and some of these people struck us as being finer personalities than some of the believers we knew. And within ourselves there was an urge, a ferment that tended to pull us away from the faith. All that is in the world – the lust of the flesh and the lust of the eyes and the pride of life – called to something within us, to something that wanted to respond. Religion, when we were young, seemed rather negative and grim, standing between us and a good time. We had left the shelter and influence of home life and had broken through the circle of home friendships into the wider world, into that world where distinctions between right and wrong are a bit blurred, and where the things most thought about and talked of are pleasure and money and material success.

It is not an easy thing to come through all that, to come through the teens and twenties with a real measure of the Christian faith in one's heart. And, in point of fact, many of your contemporaries lost it then. They began, as you did, with the advantage of a Christian home and parents and training; and then, in their teens or twenties, they took a wrong turning. Not consciously, perhaps! There was never any deliberate and definite decision against Christianity. Little by little, worldly preoccupations just smothered what faith there was in them, and today the faith has no real power to inspire them, to restrain them, to comfort them, to guide them. Some of them have got on, have got on amazingly; but would you exchange your faith for all the possessions they have won? They lost it: we have kept it.

*Would it not be truer to say that we have been kept in it?*

It would have been like Paul to say that. Faith is the

gift of God to begin with, he was wont to assert. It is wrought in us at the beginning by the Holy Spirit of God, and by the Holy Spirit it is sustained. Should we not adore and praise God, you and I, for doing this for us–for keeping us in the faith?

It is not a mere chance, a happy accident, that you and I today are not entirely worldly and unbelieving men and women, without God and without hope in this world. If today, in spite of so much worldliness and weakness in our lives, there is some real trust in God within us, some real hope through Him for this life and that which is to come, true reverence for His great name, some power within us to love Christ, to serve Him and to walk in His light; if we are men and women of Christlike principle, to God be the praise, for His Spirit has dwelt and worked within us.

I have heard that one of the Covenanters, as he walked to his death in the Grassmarket of Edinburgh, had only this to say: 'I thank God for keeping me straight.'

There would never have been that measure of Christian faith there is within us at this moment had not God by His grace shielded us, succoured us, restrained us, guided us and brought us through all we have come through, with that little divine light still burning on the altar of our hearts.

Let us give thanks to God for all that has helped to keep that light burning – for the worship of the Church that, amid the bustle and seductions of the world, has kept us in mind of realities unseen; for the sacraments when, with tenderness in our hearts, we brought our children to God or sat at the Table of the Lord, and saw there clearly the things that mattered –

felt there, in some degree, the love and grace of Christ.

Let us give thanks for words of Scripture that have had hands to pluck at our souls; for psalms and hymns round which are twined sacred and dear associations; for preachers who have strengthened our feet in the way; for books that have searched and stimulated our souls; for friends who have been God's angels in our lives; for all those ministries of God's grace whereby we have been kept in the faith.

And let us pray God to keep us walking in that light of life till travelling days are done, to make the light of faith grow within us until, for us as for Paul, it is an answer to every doubt, a continual cleansing to the conscience – the director and dynamic of our wills – the truest comfort – the abiding hope and consolation of our hearts; until we come a little nearer to saying with this Paul: 'The life which I now live in the flesh, I live by the faith of the Son of God, who loved me and gave Himself for me.'

# BLAST-OFF

## John H. Withers

*There came a sound from heaven as of a rushing mighty
wind.*                                                    Acts 2²

The New Testament account of Whit Sunday is couched
in a language and imagery quite foreign to the twentieth
century. The stage-setting of the drama in an upper room
in old Jerusalem is eerie, to say the least of it. A whistling
tornado is followed by the crackling of forked lightning,
which scatters the men from their protected seclusion
and hurls them out into the open air to begin a world
mission. However we explain it, it was the blast-off of
the Church into a new age.

How shall we explain what happened on that memorable day? Sometimes we have referred to Whit
Sunday as 'the birthday of the Church'. But surely the
Church was born on that day when Jesus called a few
men around Him at the lake shore in Galilee! Others
refer to it as 'the coming down of the Holy Spirit' – as
though now, for the first time, God's Spirit had des-
cended from some higher realm to inspire a group of
unsophisticated men and women. But this, too, makes
utter nonsense of the whole biblical revelation, in which
the Spirit of God, under many names and images, had
continually been active in human affairs. As well as
that, modern men have rejected the picture of a three-

110

tiered universe, on which the story is manifestly based – Jesus going up at the Ascension and the Holy Spirit coming down on Whit Sunday, like a celestial seesaw. We obviously need some new image to make real for us this act of God, which converted a crowd of frightened, frustrated people into a highly mobile army of witnesses, who 'turned the world upside down', and brought the Gospel of Christ's love right to the heart of a civilization.

Leaving aside for a moment the supernatural embellishments of the story, it seems to me that at the back of the whole momentous event which led to the expansion of the Church lies a sudden appreciation by the disciples of all that had happened to them since Jesus first came into their lives. Confused and stunned by His death and thrown off balance by His resurrection, which they never really anticipated, they lived in a kind of daze for several weeks. Suddenly, as we say, 'the penny dropped'; and, with a clarity which generated excitement and even hysteria, they saw some of the amazing implications of their experience of Jesus Christ. Equally important, they committed themselves to what they saw. God had been in the coming of Jesus, in the Galilean ministry, in the works of healing, even in the base betrayal and subsequent crucifixion and in the staggering fact of the Easter triumph. God had come in the total activity of Jesus to redeem humanity, to create a new society for men on the basis of a divine love. 'Holy Spirit' was their theological way of defining this action of God deep in their lives, which transformed them utterly and proposed to use them for the transformation of the world. Out of the confused adolescence of the pre-Whit Sunday experience, they suddenly 'grew up' and 'came of age'. The excitement, the mass hysteria and the speaking with tongues convinced them that a new age had dawned.

As Jews they had been conditioned to think of the Holy Spirit as 'the wind', the token of God's living activity in the world, the wind which, while itself invisible, was the cause of movement and the sign of life. 'The wind bloweth where it listeth and thou hearest the sound thereof, but canst not tell whence it cometh and whither it goeth', Jesus Himself once said. So conditioned, they experienced the movement of God's Spirit in their lives as a rushing tornado, which blew through the room of their meeting and propelled them into the world to share their good news with others and to live for others.

When, therefore, the Church sings 'Come, Holy Ghost, come as the wind', it is really a prayer that God may once more reinvigorate the Church and drive her into a Gospel to transform the whole shape of human life and society.

Several recent writers see the Spirit at work today in a movement which resembles a storm. Roger Lloyd of Winchester begins his book, *The Ferment of the Church*, with the words: 'The prospect of a new Reformation is clearly in sight. The storm signals are quite unmistakable.' The Bishop of Woolwich in his paperback, *The New Reformation?*, declares: 'There has been a troubling of the waters such as betokens the quickening of the Spirit, a rustling in the treetops.' Are we watching the beginning of a new storm of the Spirit?

Of course, a pentecostal awakening of the Church in our time will certainly not be an exact reproduction of the first Whit Sunday. But, behind this old picture of God working like a storm, I think I can detect certain great universals, which will be embodied in new forms when the Spirit moves once more to blast-off the Church in this Space Age. We can see these great universals in the lives of the early disciples.

*The Holy Spirit, God actively present in human life, swept away their crutches and they rushed out to walk by faith in obedience to the leading of God.*

Gone were the crutches on which they had been leaning for the past three years, when Jesus walked in Galilee. The Ascension was the cutting of the last physical contact with Jesus, and this was followed by Pentecost. They were now 'on their own' with no outward props to steady their convictions, no Jesus in the flesh to run to with their fears and disappointments. They had been supported by their traditional pieties, the outward trappings of their organized religion. Now the crutches were struck from under them and they walked out with no other resource than the inward conviction that the living God, the living Saviour, was the ground of their being, and in obedience to His leading they could conquer the world for truth and love. With this sudden inspiration, they embarked on a dangerous adventure which led them to the ends of the earth, always conscious of the presence of the living Christ with them. This sense of Christ's presence is the only ultimate equipment of the Christian Church.

Is not the Church today incapacitated for its real task of mission by holding on grimly to many crutches which keep it hobbling when it ought to be racing at full speed? For example, there is our deep trust in massive organizations, which become ends in themselves and greedily consume our energies and loyalties in their preservation. We have rested our faith on many traditional patterns of worship, which now seem sadly irrelevant to contemporary men. We have held on like grim death to the great dignities of the Church, forgetting that God called us, not to a position of honour but to a position of service, to minister to a world in need and to order our whole Christian community in obedience to His love. We have even invested our financial wealth, not to forward the present enterprises of the Church, but to secure the future of the organization.

Yet we are called to live by faith alone, and faith is taking the risk – or, if you like, taking Christ at His Word – that we really can walk without crutches. You remember, in St Matthew's Gospel, when Jesus sent out the twelve disciples on their first mission, He told them, 'Take no staves'. He advised the Church to throw away its props when it goes out on mission.

So, if we sincerely pray for the coming of the Holy Spirit today, we shall have to be prepared for a storm which will sweep away our many crutches: then we shall stop behaving like cripples!

*The Holy Spirit, God actively present in human life, also blew away their baggage.*

They travelled light. At the first mission recorded in the Gospel, when Jesus sent His men out two by two, He told them: 'Provide no gold, silver or copper to fill your purse, no pack for the road, no second coat, no stick.' They were soon to discover the significance of that exhortation. The Latin word for baggage is *impedimentum*, suggesting that baggage can so easily become an impediment. These first Jewish Christians were packing for their first missionary journey the rites and ceremonies of the centuries, preparing to bring with them all the Sabbath laws, the rite of circumcision, the detailed conventions of an ancient tradition. In the fifteenth chapter of the Acts of the Apostles, we find the Church, under the Spirit's inspiration, stripping itself for action and throwing aside those things which were irrelevant or even injurious to its task. The wind blew hard and the wind blew low, sweeping away their baggage like the baggage of Mary Poppins!

When we pray 'Come, Holy Ghost, come as the wind' are we prepared to let go the baggage which is 'Not Needed on Voyage'? Well – are we? Are we not carrying a great many irrelevant things which we still think necessary for the Church's survival? Many luxuries will have to be jettisoned. There is, for example, the luxury of our divisions, which some still accept as part of our survival kit. There is the luxury of out-dated theological ideas, which cut no ice in our modern secular society with its scientific presuppositions. There is the luxury of all kinds of inherited prejudices and conventions and even trivialities, which tend to isolate the Church from men of goodwill. The Spirit calls us to revival not survival. It may very well be that the Church, as we know it, will have to die that the Church of the new age may live in the Spirit of Christ.

The Bishop of Woolwich has written: 'The second Reformation will be a time of stripping down, or travelling light. The Church will go through its baggage and discover how much it can better do without, alike in doctrine and organization.' The Church must be prepared to go naked through the world, stripped of

all its pride and pretentions, accepting only such pro-
visions as God the Spirit will make for it.

*The Holy Spirit, God active in human life, blew the
disciples themselves over the frontiers of the world.*

The crutches were gone, the baggage dispersed; and,
thus lightened, the Christians themselves were blown
across many frontiers by the storm of the Holy Spirit.
The Acts of the Apostles is the record of the Church
breaking through the barriers and refusing to remain
inside the traditional frontiers, which were properly
allotted to it.

In preparation for the first missionary journey, as
recorded in St Matthew's Gospel, Jesus said to His
disciples: 'Go only to the lost sheep of the House of
Israel.' This was a necessary limitation, for, at that
stage, the disciples were merely going out on a national
experimental task – a kind of trial run. But, in the Whit
Sunday storm, the Holy Spirit swept them out of the
upper room into the market place, across the borders of
Judea into Samaria, northwards to Asia Minor, across
into Greece, and eventually to Rome itself and to the
great western empire based on it. In Acts 1 we find
Jesus speaking to the disciples: 'Ye shall be My witnesses unto the ends of the earth.'

Now, this was not merely a flight across geographical
frontiers – though it was that, and any experience of
the Spirit which does not bring with it a world mission
is surely not of Jesus Christ! – it was a blast which
carried the messengers of Christ across all frontiers.
Later on, St Paul was able to say: 'Where is neither
Jew nor Greek, Barbarian, Scythian, bond nor free;
all are one in Christ Jesus.' These early disciples were

swept across political frontiers, intellectual frontiers, racial frontiers, economic frontiers, moral frontiers. The Church, with its divine passport in its hand, was being propelled by the Holy Spirit into every realm of human activity. It was constantly taking part in 'border incidents', as it interfered in the total living of men to transform their relationships. A new pentecostal experience today will lead to the same fearless crossing of the frontiers, as Christian men and women, guided by the Spirit of Christ, bring their witness to bear in every area of human thought and activity, claiming the whole of life for the Lordship of Jesus Christ.

Sometimes, when I look at the railings around my church, I feel they are the symbol of a church in a state of siege. We have been turning in upon ourselves, preparing our positions of defence, instead of reaching out to others, to live for them, to serve them and, by the grace of God, to transform them. When Jesus said: 'The gates of hell shall not prevail against' the Church, He meant that the gates of hell, the gates of evil, could never withstand the pounding blows of a Church filled with the Holy Spirit. He intended the Church to be the aggressor. For that purpose, its members, by the power of the Spirit, must be swept across the frontiers to win the whole world.

How did it all happen? The story, as told in the Acts of the Apostles, is gloriously simple. The disciples were all together in one place, not wasting their energies and their spiritual aspirations on the things that divide and separate, but joined together in a common act of devotion to Jesus Christ, committed to serve Him and committed to proclaim His love, as sealed on the Cross, as the world's last hope. It was when, with united heart and spirit, they bowed in obedience to that living active Presence, that the Spirit came upon them, the tornado blew, the lightning forked its way from heaven to earth, and they sallied forth to conquer a world.

This was the blast-off of the Church into a new age.

*Come, Holy Ghost, come as the wind!*

# OUR UNRESTRICTED GOD

## A. SKEVINGTON WOOD

*And there came a man of God, and spake unto the king of
Israel, and said, Thus saith the Lord, Because the Syrians
have said, The Lord is God of the hills, but He is not God
of the valleys, therefore will I deliver all this great
multitude into thine hand, and ye shall know that I am
the Lord.* I Kings 20[28]

This text opens with a quotation. It tells us what the
Syrians thought about the God of Israel. Since they had
not received the revelation that had been granted to the
Hebrews, theirs represents an inadequate conception.
This is the best men can do in trying to define the nature
of God when they rely solely upon their own judgement.
They cannot by searching find out the truth concerning
Him. God is known only as He chooses to disclose
Himself. Whatever conclusions men reach of their own
accord are bound to be unsatisfactory.

In this case the Syrians in their blindness decided that
God was restricted in His capacity. He was a God of the
hills but not of the valleys. They and their armies had
just been roundly defeated at the siege of Samaria.
But they seized on a ready excuse for their failure and
buoyed themselves up with false hopes for the future.
The God of Israel, they persuaded themselves, was
essentially a God of the hills, and that accounted for

119

His success on the heights of Samaria. The ancient world was accustomed to local deities associated with some natural feature like a mountain or a stream. This God of the Hebrews, the Syrians concluded, was a hill God. They probably knew next to nothing about the worship of Israel; but, if they had picked up a shred or two of evidence, it might have confirmed their theory, in that Jehovah had manifested Himself to His people more than once on the mountain-top and that His temple was in Jerusalem, a city set on a hill. Samaria, as we have seen, was similarly located and this circumstance provided the Syrians with a convenient excuse to save face. They therefore planned to challenge the Israelites next time on the plain and felt confident that victory would be theirs. A God of the hills would be helpless in the valley.

So the Syrians argued, and we know now how mistaken they were. It is easy, however, to be wise after the event, and we must not consider them too foolish because we are more enlightened. Indeed, we must not overlook the fact that many today subscribe to this Syrian misconception of God. Most people who believe in God at all agree that He is a God of the hills. He makes Himself known in the high places of spiritual experience. He comes into His own on the mountain-peak, where man seeks to realize the loftiest aspirations of his soul. But there is an extraordinarily persistent notion that somehow the valleys are out of God's domain. It is felt that the more normal levels of life are excluded from His oversight or interest. When we speak of God's providence, we mean, in ninety-nine cases out of a hundred, something huge and spectacular, not the humble and familiar.

Nor is this simply the tendency of the unbeliever or the formal Christian. It is a failing even of the keenest and most zealous. Genuinely regenerated and indubitably earnest children of God may nevertheless fall for this fallacy at some time or other. We are tempted to associate the activity of Almighty God exclusively with the striking and unusual occasions of life, and virtually banish Him from the realm of the routine and ordinary. Even in Christian service we are waiting for some special assignment, when we should be tackling the task nearest at hand, however trivial and unexciting it may appear. In the words of the hymn, we are always 'seeking for some great thing to do or secret thing to know'. We think that Christianity is no more than a glut of emotional ecstasies. We crave continually for the mountain top and forget that the humdrum valley belongs also to the Lord. It may be that God is about to challenge us through this Old Testament text. Like Naaman, we need to be taught that what is required of us is not 'some great thing', but obedience and faith in that which seems small and unimportant.

There are three salient features of this highly illuminating verse.

*The first is the limitation of unbelief.*

The Syrians had only a restricted view of God. Because they were pagans, their outlook was narrow and cramping. They lacked the breadth that comes with faith.

This is not how we usually think of the distinction between belief and unbelief. This is certainly not how unbelievers think of themselves. They imagine that theirs is the wider canvas. They are always complaining about the restraints imposed by faith. They like to suppose that theirs is the broader viewpoint and that, as a result, life for them is richer and fuller. Nothing could be further from the facts. No life is so narrow as that which is hemmed in by unbelief. Nothing is more restrictive than sin.

Some years ago now, Prebendary J. B. Phillips, whose New Testament paraphrase is so often used and justly popular, wrote a book with a most challenging title. It was directed at those who reject the fullness of the Christian Gospel. Its caption was this: *Your God is too Small*. That is what happens when men discard the revelation of Scripture. They are compelled to live in a shrunken world. For our view of God necessarily colours our view of life. That is why the fool who says in his heart that there is no God is confronted by a vast emptiness. He is left with what H. G. Wells called a 'God-shaped blank' in his soul, which projects itself into an image of the environment in which he is set.

Recently, I have been reading a fascinating spiritual autobiography by Yvonne Lubbock. She was a musician of no mean talents – a pupil of Myra Hess – who married a Cambridge don and settled down to domestic life, interspersed with literary outbursts. Being put off in youth by a worthless nominal churchianity, she sought refuge in agnosticism until she came to realize what a miserable, inhibiting thing it is. Even the boasted intellectual honesty of her rationalist friends she found in some instances to consist in saying what they thought without having taken the trouble to think. It was in the quest for life and liberty that eventually she escaped from the limitation of unbelief and came to find satisfaction and fulfilment in the God and Father of our

Lord Jesus Christ. Now she is a Christian and enjoys the spaciousness of faith.

When we come to consider it more deeply, to claim that God, if He exists at all, belongs to the hills but is quite unsuited to the valleys, is to make a most sweeping assertion. Agnosticism may sound like modesty, but it is in fact an outrageous conceit as well as a logical contradiction. 'If you say that man is too little for God to speak to him,' declared Blaise Pascal, 'you must be very big to be able to judge.' Who are we indeed to determine the extent of God's sovereignty? If we rush to the hasty conclusion that He is confined to the hills, we shall discover to our cost, as the Syrians did, that He reigns in the valleys also, and that, wherever we may hide, we are still answerable to Him.

*That leads us to the second feature of this text. It is the emancipation of faith.*

To arrive at a true view of God as revealed in Jesus Christ our Lord is to be liberated into the wealthy place of peace and joy. 'Thou hast set my feet in a large room,' the Psalmist declares. And again: 'I called upon the Lord in distress: the Lord answered me, and set me in a large place.' When we are led to trust in God, we are freed from the prison-house to enjoy the glorious liberty of His children in which all things are ours in Christ. As Thomas Traherne put it, the sea itself flows in our veins, we are clothed with the heavens, and crowned with the stars. All space and all time belong to us because we are in Christ and He is its Lord.

Not far from the place where the Syrians had suffered their setbacks, our Lord Jesus Christ once talked to a woman by a well. He taught her that God is not of the hills only, by any manner of means. 'Our fathers worshipped in this mountain (that, is Gerizim, the headquarters of the Samaritan cult); and ye say (that is, as a Jew) that in Jerusalem is the place where men ought to worship.' Note the drift of her argument: 'God is the God of the hills', she is saying in effect, 'but which hill is it to be – Gerizim or Zion?' Now our Lord's reply makes it plain beyond all question that God is the God of the valleys as well as of the hills. To borrow the terms used by the Bishop of Woolwich in his controversial book, *Honest to God*, He is 'down here' as well as 'up there'. 'Woman, believe Me, the hour cometh, when ye shall neither in this mountain, nor yet at Jerusalem, worship the Father. . . But the hour cometh, and now is, when the true worshippers shall worship the Father in spirit and in truth, for the Father seeketh such to worship Him. God is a Spirit.'

All this makes the Incarnation even more astonishing than we had suspected it to be. Archbishop Temple once said that no one had a right to believe in the Incarnation at all who had not first found it incredible. And the more firmly we recognize that ours is the God of the hills of heaven, the more amazing it appears that ever He should stoop to make Himself known down here in the valleys of earth. Yet this is just what He did in Jesus Christ our Lord. The wonder of it should never be allowed to fade from our hearts.

Russell Maltby, that much-loved Methodist figure here in Britain, once had a long talk with an unbeliever who was beginning to realize the miracle of the Gospel. In the end, after the Doctor had told the simple story of how God so loved the world that He gave His only-begotten Son, the man confessed: 'Well, I still don't know whether it is true or not that God came down to earth for us men and for our salvation, but I do know that it is the most beautiful thought that ever entered the mind of man.' 'Then,' asked Maltby eagerly, 'aren't you prepared to believe that God might think that, too?'

Here is the supreme paradox of the Christian faith: it was the divine concentration of God in Christ which made possible our emancipation into the large place of faith and hope and love. Henceforth we know that this Gospel of ours has to do with the valleys as well as with the hills. Our Christianity must be lived out down here, on 'the dull plains of earth'. We are to live as Christ lived where He lived – in this present evil world. That is the inescapable context of Christian witness.

*But there is a further and final feature of this text. It is the demonstration of reality.*

The verse before us sets two sayings in apposition. The Syrians claimed: 'The Lord is God of the hills, but He is not God of the valleys.' But God declared: 'Therefore will I deliver all this great multitude into thine hand, and ye shall know that I am the Lord.' The matter was to be put to the proof. God was about to demonstrate that He was as powerful in the valley as on the hill. At Aphek, down on the plain, He gave the Israelites a victory as decisive as on the heights of Samaria. We read that one hundred thousand Syrian infantrymen were slain in one day and another twenty-seven thousand, who fled into the city for refuge, were involved in total disaster when a great wall collapsed upon them. God showed Himself as good as His Word. He gave victory in the valley as well as on the hilltop.

That is what He is waiting to do in your life and mine.

He knows what your particular valley may be. It could be the valley of fear. It could be the valley of depression. It could be the valley of temptation. It could be the valley of moral defeat. Whatever it is, God is God there and will enable you to come off more than conqueror in His love. There is no situation too big for Him. In all things He is able. He is 'El Shaddai' – the 'Enough' God. Dr Campbell Morgan has told us that the title means quite literally 'the Mighty One of Resource and Sufficiency'. The word is related to that which means a breast. To a baby, the mother is all-sufficient. At her breast he nestles and draws his sustenance. The child of God finds in Him all he needs. There is 'enough for all, enough for each, enough for evermore'. Ample provision has been made in Christ and through the Holy Spirit for a life of victory.

One of the great stalwarts of Methodist mission work in the recent past was Charles H. Hulbert. His life-story has been written by his son, and carries a significant title, *Passion for Souls*. In the Foreword, Dr W. E. Sangster describes Hulbert as 'singleminded, with an undeviating aim to bring others to the Saviour'. He spent thirty-three years of his ministry in eight Central Halls, and filled every one of them. Then in 1937 he was separated as a Connexional Evangelist and was instrumental in the conversion of many, as he had been consistently throughout his superintendencies. Hulbert was a stirring preacher, but no message of his made a more striking impact on his hearers than his vivid sermon on 'Gods and Lions'. It was based on the question put by King Darius to the prophet Daniel after his night in the lions' den. We read in Scripture that the monarch 'cried with a lamentable voice'. We

can understand the reason why. Doubtless he feared
that Daniel was no more, and that the only answer he
would receive to his inquiry would be the roar of a
contented animal. 'O Daniel, servant of the living God,'
he asked, 'is thy God whom thou servest continually,
able to deliver thee from the lions?'

In his sermon, Hulbert would line up the gods man
worships – pleasure, power, fame, wealth, and the like,
and measure them against the lions that seek his soul to
devour it – greed and lust and pride and every sort of
subtle sin. With piercing logic he would show that the
false gods in which man places his trust are insufficient
to deliver him from the lions which lie in wait at every
turn. The only God who is worth serving, he would
conclude, is one who is bigger than the lions, and that is
the Lord God Almighty whom Daniel chose. 'My God
hath sent His angel, and hath shut the lions' mouths,
that they have not hurt me.' That was the surprising
reply Darius received, and it led him to publish a further
decree: 'That in every dominion of my kingdom men
tremble and fear before the God of Daniel: for He is
the living God, and stedfast for ever, and His kingdom
that which shall not be destroyed, and His dominion
shall be even unto the end. He delivereth and rescueth,
and He worketh signs and wonders in heaven and in
earth, who hath delivered Daniel from the power of
the lions.'

We live in an age which tends to devalue God. What
may be regarded as reduced views of His nature and
capacities are much in vogue. But we must remember
that if we are to be really honest to God, we must be
honest to His Word, and take our conception of Him
from what is revealed there. What kind of a God are

you envisaging and serving today? Is He the God of the speculative theologians, or the God of the Bible? Is He the God who cannot or the God who can? Is He able to deliver you from the lions which beset you? Is he only a god of the hills who leaves you in the lurch down in the valley where you need him most? Or is your trust in the living and true God, the God who is able to deliver you from the power of the lions, the God of the valleys as well as the hills, the God and Father of our Lord and Saviour Jesus Christ, the God who gave His Son to die on the Cross so that those who look to Him for salvation might have life for evermore? When Christ is ours, this God is ours. There is no other way, for it was our Lord Himself who solemnly assured us that no man can come to the Father but by Him. Only in Christ, and yet confidently in Christ, can we repeat these stupendous lines of Isaac Watts:

> *The God that rules on high,*
> *That all the earth surveys,*
> *That rides upon the stormy sky,*
> *And calms the roaring seas:*
> *This aweful God is ours,*
> *Our Father and our love:*
> *He will send down His heavenly powers,*
> *To carry us above.*

# TREASURE IN EARTHEN VESSELS

### GERALD KENNEDY

*But we have this treasure in earthen vessels, to show that the transcendent power belongs to God and not to us.*
2 Corinthians 4[7]

There is an old legend about the early days of the race when men gathered around the fire at night for protection and safety. They told stories about the events of the day and the experiences of the hunt. There was one member of the tribe who was not a good hunter and not a very skilful man in any of the common activities. But he had a great gift of words and he could tell stories about what had happened and the adventures his brethren had experienced. As they put it: 'The words came alive and marched up and down in the hearts of the hearers.' After a while some of the elders became concerned at the great power this man had with his words. 'After we are gone,' they said among themselves, 'he may tell lies about us.' So they killed him, only to find when it was too late that the magic was not in the man but in the word.

Something of this recognition is being set forth to us in these words of St Paul. He is saying to his generation and to ours that the magic is not in men. We are, he says, but earthen vessels, easily broken and not long-lasting. Anything we have of great value is from God

129

who entrusts His treasures to our keeping for a while. The greatness of men, in other words, is not in themselves but in what they say, what they stand for, what they believe.

Until we come to terms with what men are, we are in no position to describe what we may expect from them. We have tended to neglect the biblical anthropology while giving most of our attention to biblical theology. This is not to say that we should neglect what we have done but that we must pay more attention to the biblical word about man. If I were looking for a single statement which sums it up best, I would choose this affirmation of St Paul. Here is the truth about man. Everything goes right with us if we remember it and everything goes wrong with us if we forget it. The evils of our time have their roots in a false interpretation of humanity and until we have come to terms with the truth about human nature, all is in vain.

Let us look with some care, therefore, at Paul's insight into the nature of man.

*We may begin by suggesting that a great many people hope that we will create a race of supermen.*

This idea, associated with Nietzsche, is really rather commonplace in the thinking of our contemporaries. Just the other day I read of a scientist predicting we shall learn how to increase the size of our brain which will give us the ability to deal with the computer machines we are constructing. Our cry is for more intelligence and we assume that if we could become smart enough we could solve our problems.

The literature written around the beginning of the French Revolution amazes us with its confidence in human reason. The Enlightenment was a hopeful move in the direction of salvation by brain. When we read some of the discourses set forth by eighteenth-century thinkers, we are amazed at their optimism and hope. They believed sincerely that once men were free from the shackles of class and allowed to follow their own bent without interference, they would create a heaven on earth. The natural goodness of humanity was lifted up to the exclusion of any recognition of sin and corruption, and it was bliss to be alive. What a terrible disillusionment it is to see the Revolution deteriorate into the Terror and become a pattern of madness more appropriate in an insane asylum than in a free nation!

In our time we have thought of science as the instrument which would set us free from limitations and mistakes. With the delicate instruments of precision we can do so many things and provide so many advantages. I read the other day that science has a machine which can weigh a book and measure the difference of five words. Surely this means science is the road to heaven!

In our own lifetime we have gone from the hopefulness of scientific optimism to the pessimism of scientific despair. For out of this method and power have come the instruments of destruction and the threat of annihilation. Sometimes it seems as if in science we have a tiger by the tail dragging us over the abyss, but we dare not let go. There was a day when men talked about a moratorium on preaching and today there are many who secretly wish that there could be a moratorium on science.

It is Communist heresy which assumes that the new

heaven and the new earth will come to us by way of intelligence. When Lenin and his followers cut themselves off from religion, they cut themselves off from the truth about human nature. They went back to the Enlightenment as the answer to human problems. Some of the books being smuggled out of Russia telling the story of life under the Soviets do not seem to be descriptions of Utopia. The corruption of men is as apparent among Communists as it is among Capitalists.

Is it true that delinquency is simply a matter of under-privilege and poverty? Sometimes it is rooted in such things, but in our time our delinquents so often come from the right side of the avenue and from homes of over-privilege. We are wise when we try to fight poverty, but we are foolish if we think that the elimination of poverty means all will be well with us. One of the most disturbing things we face is bright young people with every material advantage who are morally sick.

We live up above the Hollywood Bowl, and one summer Sunday morning we passed the entrance to the Bowl on our way to a church where I was preaching. Young people were waiting at the gate of the Bowl, which would not open until late afternoon. When we returned from church, we saw youngsters climbing around the hills above the Bowl and people were in cars parked along the roads too far away either to see or hear what was going on. That night the Beatles arrived, and now and again we could hear a great scream which sounded like nothing so much as a tribal frenzy being built up deliberately by a medicine man. What was going on? Four young men who needed haircuts and have mildly pleasant voices were singing – or trying to; and I said to myself that it does not look as if this generation has made any notable progress towards solving their problems by intelligence.

The educated man is in a sense the real threat of our time. He is the one who has developed his brain and increased his intelligence until he can use crowds and concentrate power in himself. Whatever else may be said about dictatorship, it knows how to use brilliant men to create tyranny.

This must mean that there is a vast section of human life which education cannot reach. A man is not just a brain and a man is never entirely a rational creature. Those who imagine that bringing men into the Kingdom is merely a matter of increasing their thinking ability are on the wrong track. The education of the mind is important enough, but when the heart is left a jungle of primitive emotions, more education means more danger and a graver threat to the common life.

I must confess that I understand very little about the Laser beam. I know only that in some marvellous way it uses light to perform wonders of healing. It can be a weapon in man's fight against disease and darkness. But some time ago I saw that the Laser rifle can be used to kill and destroy. And I thought to myself: Can it be true that light which symbolizes man's hope can actually be used as a weapon to destroy man? Apparently even light can be turned against man, and in some way this is the greatest disillusionment of all. Those who believe that we can increase our intelligence and be saved by supermen are victims of a false hope and doomed to utter disillusionment.

*We may move from this high concept and accept one which is too low. We can say that man is evil and must be ruled.*

Those who take this tack will say that men are little higher than the beasts and are the victims of their wild, uncontrolled impulses. The answer is to recognize this and discipline men. Such men see freedom as an impossible idea and something which we do not want and are incapable of using wisely.

This, of course, is the Fascist philosophy which we saw in action during World War II. When men saw what this means, they knew suddenly that this was not what they wanted. The heroism of the early forties was called into being by a vision of a nightmare world controlled for its own good by self-appointed masters.

We see the same philosophy at work in the economic exploitation of colonial peoples. The theory is that if people have not reached the proper level of culture and civilization, they must be ruled and used. Some of the strange antics of the newly-free nations of Africa bear witness that it is a long road to self-discipline and self-control. Fascism may insist that certain races are innately inferior and must draw the water and hew the wood for the masters.

When this idea takes hold of men, it sometimes turns even great scholars into propagandists. Professor William Albright, the famous archaeologist, points out that such a tragedy overcame two German scholars, Kittel and Fischer. Fischer was a scientist, an authority on human genetics, and Kittel was a leading Protestant scholar and theologian. These two men, captured by the dream of national socialism in Germany, deserted their scholarly discipline and collaborated on a book which brought blushes to the cheeks of every scholar in the field. Listen to these words of Albright:

In many ways Kittel and Fischer typified European intellectual activity at its best, since the two men were leaders in their philological and biological fields. Surrendering to the devil of intellectual over-confidence, they plunged into the uncharted depths between their respective islands of special skill. Selling themselves to Satan, they abandoned the Judeo-Christian tradition of the Fatherhood of God and the brotherhood of man. Worshipping at the shrine of the ancient pagan gods of *Blut und Boden*, they adopted the mark of Cain as their perpetual badge of dishonour. And what happened in Germany can take place wherever human intellect turns its back on the spiritual traditions which we have inherited from their sources in ancient Israel.

(William Foxwell Albright, *History, Archaeology and Christian Humanism*, New York, McGraw-Hill, 1964.)

Thus did these scholars sell themselves to men seeking some intellectual excuse to persecute the Jews.

This same danger is manifest when men distrust the physical part of life. Sometimes in the name of a superior spirituality, they regard the body as intrinsically evil and adopt the Greek doctrine of body and spirit in constant, inevitable warfare. St Paul pictured the body as a temple of the Holy Spirit, and only when we remember this truth can we remain healthy.

If sex is regarded as an evil thing in itself, then the monasteries become centres of a superior religious experience because marriage is repudiated. Sex that is thus repressed breaks out every now and then in evil excesses, because it is one of the powerful impulses God has given men. The biblical teaching is that all of life is sacred. Whenever we despise a part of it, we have failed to understand the truth about ourselves.

There was a small fundamentalist college somewhere in the middle west of America that advertised it was seven miles from any known form of sin. If I could believe that there was any place I could go that would get me seven miles away from sin, I would go there as fast as possible. I would apply for a job on the faculty of such a college; and, if refused, I would be glad to be a caretaker. But, of course, all this is nonsense. If it is true that man is not above all evil, it is true also that he cannot live his life subjugating any impulse that may lead to evil.

*Paul's word is that man's treasure is in earthen vessels.*

He may roam the heavens, but his feet are made of clay. He is capable of the best and of the worst, and in his person he bears the mark of greatness and the stain of depravity.

This means, I think, that man is a symbol of something both a part of him and beyond him. The significant thing about us is what we believe. There was a time when we suggested that it makes no difference what we believe if we are sincere. We were looking not only for a religionless Christianity but a creedless Christianity. All of this is nonsense, for we are shaped and our destiny is determined by what we dare to believe.

On Sunday morning in most churches there is a time when the congregation stands together and repeats the Creed. It may be a modern affirmation of faith or the Apostles' Creed. We do it perfunctorily usually, but this is one of the greatest moments of worship and one of the greatest experiences in human life. When a congregation stands and says: 'I believe in God the Father Almighty, Maker of heaven and earth' that is a great moment. For in that act we confess our allegiance to something beyond the world and to One whose ways are not our ways. Only man can do this and only man can proclaim his faith in values far beyond himself.

Our greatness comes out of what we stand for. How often I have seen this in my ministry! I look at ordinary people without exceptional gifts whose lives have become symbols of the undying and the everlasting. This is what Paul was talking about when he wrote to the Ephesians: 'Therefore take the whole armour of God, that you may be able to withstand in the evil day, and having done all, to stand' (Ephesians 6[13]). We may be earthen vessels indeed, but we have been given the power to incarnate greatness.

Our nature is determined by what and whom we serve. If we bear the sign of the King, it marks us as creatures who bear eternal treasure within earthen vessels. This came to me a few years ago when I met an elderly bishop of our church. After years of service in Africa, he retired in the U.S.A. and attended meetings of our Council. He had a tendency to wander a bit when he spoke and there was nothing in his words of drama or excitement. And then I went to Africa myself and my eyes were opened. I learned how years ago this man and his wife had walked the trails up through the Congo jungle. I went to small villages where an old man or an old woman would inquire through the interpreter if I knew Bishop Springer. Then they would tell about how young Dr Springer had come there years ago and told the story of his Master. It came to me that this man was full of wonder and light because he had dedicated his service to Christ. Treasure in an earthen vessel, indeed!

This is a paradox which in some ways is very confusing to the world. For, on the one hand, the Christian is haughtier than all others and takes a higher point of view toward himself and his brethren. Then, just as we are getting ready to talk about Christian pride, we see in him the humbleness, the humility, that comes from a frank recognition of his own sins and mistakes. The Christian is very humble about himself and very proud of what he represents and whom he serves.

There is no wailing sadness in the Christian about man. You will find the Christian discouraged about his own sins at times and weeping over his own unworthiness. But about man who has been made a little lower than the angels, he takes a very high view and will insist that no man is to be treated as less than a son of God.

The Christian will not fall into some fad like Christian Science or Gnosticism. He will not believe that all evil is appearance and he will not believe in a superior knowledge that sets him above evil. He must, on the contrary, keep clear in his mind that evil is real enough and succeeds too often in overcoming good human impulses. But he keeps coming back to the insight of St Paul that this earthen vessel is worthy of honour because it contains a divine treasure.

One of my friends, the late Dr Roy L. Smith, said that he went to college by a great sacrifice of his parents. He had won the broad jump in a track-meet that first year and when he came home this was all he could talk about. In vain his mother tried to find out what he had learned and what new ideas had come to him. But all he could do was boast of his athletic victory. One day as they rode together out across the Kansas prairie, a jack-rabbit came out of a bush, ran across the road and disappeared. His mother said quietly: 'Roy, that jack-rabbit never went to college and it can jump farther than you can!' Roy got the point and realized that college was not primarily to make him an athlete, but to do something for his mind and his spirit. Physically, we are but earthen vessels, but spiritually we can contain the eternal treasures of God.

*Finally, let us rejoice that God triumphs through our weaknesses.*

It is good news for ordinary folks that some of the greatest treasures have come from very plain vessels. Rabbi Joshua was once taunted by an emperor's daughter because of his mean appearance. He pointed to the earthen jars which contained her father's finest wines. Whereupon she placed the wine in silver vessels, but it turned sour. The rabbi then taught her that humble vessels sometimes contain the greatest treasure.

I think of the young woman who will never be Miss California or Miss America or Miss Universe. In spite of TV's propaganda that nothing can happen to the girl who has not learned all the beauty tricks, life is still more than a surface prettiness. She may find the inner beauty which increases with every passing year. She may learn a happiness deeper than the poor young woman who thinks that the earthen vessel is all there is to it. Or here is the young man who will never be in the movies. No one will ever ask him to model for a shirt, but let him learn that God has great treasure to bestow upon any man who can accept it.

This is the meaning of the Incarnation. Isaiah spoke of 'a Man of sorrows and acquainted with grief'. He wrote about One who had no comeliness and from whom people would turn their faces. Let us never forget the mystery and the wonder of God coming to us through a man. And what a Man he was! Tempted as we are tempted and treated not as royalty but as scum, He was denied the ordinary securities of life and knew little about the comforts of living. Finally, He died in anguish and pain to say to us that these earthen vessels we call our bodies reflect the glory of God. Martin Luther had the courage to suggest that each man could be an incarnation and ought to be as Christ to his neighbour. This is good news.

An American was worshipping one Sunday morning in one of the largest Protestant churches of Dresden in East Germany. He reports that during the service he was astonished to hear the pastor pray for the mayor of Dresden, the district governor of Saxony, and the head of the East German régime – all Communists. After the service he asked about it. The pastor reminded him gently that St Paul in Romans exhorts Christians to pray for their rulers who were persecuting them and would one day execute St Paul. 'And besides,' the pastor said quietly, 'when I pray for the mayor it reminds him that he is not God.'

Oh, let no man believe that he can become wise enough to be a god! Let us never be corrupted by the teaching that some men are to be ruled and used by wiser men. But let us rejoice in St Paul's word that we have treasure in earthen vessels and remember who we are. For in this word there is our salvation and our joy.

# ON BEING FINELY AWARE AND RICHLY RESPONSIBLE

ROBERT J. MCCRACKEN

*On entering the house of Peter, Jesus noticed that his mother-in-law was down with fever.*     Matthew 8[14]

He noticed! That was characteristic of Him. Wherever He went His alert eye took in all that was happening. There are people who move in and out among their neighbours wearing blinkers; there is a great deal they fail to notice; they are oblivious to the diversity and desperateness of human need. They are detached and unobservant because they are self-absorbed. It was never so with Jesus. He entered into the lives of people, He put Himself in their place, saw with their eyes, felt what they were feeling. Intuitively, with a rare clairvoyance, He realized their problems, sensed their needs, reached out to them a helping hand.

To live in such fashion is expensive. To have a responsive, understanding heart is not, as one goes through life, to tread a primrose path. Yet fellow-feeling and self-involvement are deeply satisfying. It is a great thing to be fully wherever you are, and not, in mind, somewhere else. The self-absorbed frequently are somewhere else. It is a great thing to be keenly aware of the people round about you, the people with whom you are living and working, to notice how things are with them, whether they are up or down, sick or well, sad or merry. It is a great thing to keep the imagination alive, the capacity for feeling strong, not to allow sympathy and tenderness to be blunted, in Henry James's phrase, to be 'finely aware and richly responsible'.

Life can be a toughening process. This is why those of you who are young have to watch what happens to your ideals – those you cherish about yourself, the work you plan to do, the home you have in mind to make, the contribution you can offer to your country as a citizen. Ideals are native to youth. If you don't have them in the twenties, if the *status quo* doesn't anger you, if you are not a crusader now for some just cause, some sorely needed and overdue reform, what in heaven's name will you be like in what could be the fat forties? Even if you do have ideals, even if in your late teens and twenties you participate in debates, pass resolutions, join societies, protest against nuclear testing, take part in sit-ins and teach-ins, shock your parents by your radicalism, you will require as you grow older to be on your guard against two subtle and corroding tendencies – one of them compromise and the other cynicism.

The middle years are the testing time. It is not uncommon for idealism about one's marriage, one's profession, one's politics, one's church membership to give way to disillusionment, then scepticism, then cynicism, then apathy. A college president asked an alumnus: 'What are you in business for?' Without a trace of embarrassment the alumnus replied: 'To make my little pile and then get out.' Can you imagine that alumnus in his undergraduate years? Hotly dissatisfied – or so one would like to think – with the world as he found it. Confident that he could do something to help set it to rights. But see him in the middle fifties – the organization man, fleshy, easy-going, accommodating himself without discomfort or strain to the world and its ways. John Kennedy said he was told by an old hand when he entered Congress: 'The way to get along is to go along.' That way compromise weds with cynicism, and one by one ideals go down the drain. That way a person ceases to be 'loyal to the royal' in himself and becomes brittle and *blasé*. Give him a few years and he scoffs at idealism, says idealists have their heads in the clouds, that they are dreamers, visionaries, and prides himself on being a realist who can get things done directly, swiftly, competently, without pious platitudes.

Life can be a toughening process. The longer men and women live the harder they can become. Because to be finely aware and richly responsible is expensive, they can grow a protective shell about themselves, a shell so thick that self-interest becomes the one spring of action and the gratification of the senses the chief end of life. A novelist summed up one of his characters in a sentence: 'Edith was a little country bounded on the north, south, east and west by Edith.' A man from the Middle West put an advertisement in the newspaper which read: 'I am fifty-eight years old. Would like to marry a young woman of thirty who has a tractor. Please send a picture of the tractor.' What had happened to Edith and the farmer is obvious. They had allowed life to narrow their interests. They were wrapped up in themselves. As types they are extreme, but they illustrate a tendency that exerts pressure on all of us. There are good respectable people by the thousand who have ceased to notice, who no longer care greatly or feel deeply – husbands living year after year with their wives and never really discovering with whom they are living, what goes on in their heads and hearts, what life means to them, or what they want from it; parents with children growing up in their homes whom they do not really notice or know; good respectable people in whom imagination has died, whose sympathies have become so contracted that their judgements are incredibly prejudiced and harsh. When Muriel Lester was twelve years old and appalled by the sight of the slums of London, her well-to-do father, full of solicitude for her, said: 'It's all right. They don't feel things the same way as we do. And if they did, they've only got themselves to blame. They get drunk. That's why they're so poor.' A man, you see, with a protective shell around him, trying to put one round his daughter. He meant well but, thank God, he didn't succeed. Muriel Lester grew up to be a woman finely aware and richly responsible.

The trouble with the lives of multitudes is not that they are vicious, but that they are so often trivial. It is not that they are guilty of any flagrant evil, but that gradually and insensibly they become immersed in narrow, petty, self-regarding concerns. A man made himself famous in the catering business. He established a chain of restaurants right across the American continent. As he lay dying, his relatives gathered round his bed. They bent over him to hear his final words. His last whisper was: 'Slice the ham thin.' You laugh. It could be that you laughed too soon. It could be that you are laughing at yourself. Do you happen to know Phyllis McGinley's poem 'Occupation Housewife'? It is a poem about what can happen to a woman in the middle years.

*Her health is good. She owns to forty-one,*
  *Keeps her hair bright with vegetable rinses,*
*Has two well-nourished children – daughter and son,*
  *Just now away at school. Her house, with chintzes,*
*Expensive, curtained, animates the caller,*
  *And she is fond of early American glass,*
*Stacked in an English breakfront, somewhat taller*
  *Than her best friend's. Last year she took a class*
*In modern drama at the County Centre.*
  *Twice on Good Fridays she's heard 'Parsifal' sung.*
*She often says she might have been a painter,*
  *Or writer, perhaps, except she married young.*
*She diets, and with Contract she delays*
*The encroaching desolation of her days.*

The sting is in the last line – 'the encroaching desolation of her days'. Time and time again it is clear as daylight why people are disillusioned about life and bored by it. They are not expendable. They are hoarding what they should be giving away. They are fussing over themselves – their health, their diet, their figure, the impression they make on others – when, with their education, background, opportunities, they should be spending themselves, devoting their time, skills, money to people and causes. They think they are here to be served. They are wrong. They are here to serve.

Dr Benjamin Tenney, a Boston surgeon, said this: 'It has taken me half my life to discover that my business in the world is not to try to make something of myself, but rather to find a job worth doing and lose myself in it.' This is what it means to be finely aware and richly responsible. It is to get out of your own light. It is to cease measuring existence in terms of what it gives, or does not give you. It is to care greatly and feel deeply. It is to expand your interests and push out your horizons. It is not to keep out of things but to get into things that are worthwhile. It is to resolve decade by decade to put more into life than you take out. 'The first and greatest of all the commandments is: Thou shalt care for the Lord thy God with all thy heart, and with all thy soul, and with all thy mind, and with all thy strength. And the second is like unto it: Thou shalt care for thy neighbour as thyself.'

We are close here to a secret – to what in life gives the deepest satisfaction. It is not success, prestige, property, money. People have had one or other or all of these and have been downright miserable. It is spending life for something that will outlast it. It is being used for a purpose which you recognize as a worthy one. It is forgetting yourself, letting yourself go out to friends, interests, causes. As to that, Jesus said the definitive word: 'Whoever will save his life will lose it; and whoever will lose his life for My sake will find it.' It is the language of paradox, but experience keeps on verifying it as true. Life finds its real utterance, climbs to its loftiest levels, not in protecting the self, coddling, and shielding it, but in the fullness of personal relationships, in self-forgetfulness, in caring for others.

Something that Schweitzer wrote he might have written expressly for Americans: 'You are happy, therefore you are called upon to give much. Whatever more than others you have received in health, natural gifts, working capacity, success, a beautiful childhood, harmonious family circumstances, you must not accept as being a matter of course. You must pay a price for them. You must show more than average devotion of life to life.'

What is the price? Miriam Teichner provides an answer:

> *God – let me be aware.*
> *Stab my soul fiercely awake with others' pain,*
> *Let me walk seeing horror and stain.*
> *Let my hands, groping, find other hands.*
> *Give me the heart that divines, understands.*
> *Give me the courage, wounded, to fight.*
> *Flood me with knowledge, drench me in light.*
> *Please, keep me eager just to do my share.*
> *God – let me be aware.*

# 'LET'S CELEBRATE!'

## David A. MacLennan

*Then I saw an angel flying in mid-heaven, with an eternal gospel to proclaim to those who dwell on earth, to every nation and tribe, language and people. He cried in a loud voice: 'Reverence God, and give glory to Him; for the hour of His judgement has come! Worship Him who made heaven, and earth, the sea and the springs of water!'*

Revelation 14[6-7]

'Let's celebrate!' It is what we say when a happy event has occurred, or some joy has come to a member of the family or to one of our friends. 'Let's celebrate' when a war ends, when some long-sought-for reform has been accepted. An event which brings joy is the reason for our celebration.

When we look at a dictionary we may be surprised that this is not the original meaning of 'celebrate'. When first used in the English language it meant 'to perform publicly and with due form (any religious ceremony) . . . to observe with solemn rites . . . to make publicly known'. In one of these meanings the Church spoke of celebrating the Eucharist, the Lord's Supper, Holy Communion. To many Protestants the use of the word 'celebrate' in connection with the Lord's Supper seems foreign and inappropriate. Many in the Reformed branches of the Christian Church would ask: 'But we do not celebrate, do we? We administer the Sacrament or we partake of the Sacrament.' 'Administer' or 'partake' are proper terms.

Today, however, I would like you to think of our right, indeed our obligation, to *celebrate* the Thanksgiving Meal of the Church. The chosen Scripture is from the strange, often puzzling and cryptic, book of the Revelation of St John. You will remember that the prophet John has been imprisoned because of his loyalty to Christ. He is writing this letter to the young churches, to tell them to keep steadfast in their loyalty to their leader and Lord, the exalted Christ. He relates visions or dreams he has had which he hopes convey to his readers the meaning of the conflict, of the cost of discipleship and assurance of the ultimate victory of God over all the forces of evil.

In the fourteenth chapter there are these words:

Then I saw an angel flying in mid-heaven, with an eternal gospel to proclaim to those who dwell on earth, to every nation and tribe, language and people. He cried in a loud voice: 'Reverence God, and give glory to Him, for the hour of His judgement has come! Worship Him who made heaven and earth, the sea and the springs of water!'

The author of this book remembered that the Gospel comes as an invitation to all mankind. In the midst of his vivid and sometimes grotesque pictures of the completion of the grand design of God, he pictures an angel – a ministering servant with an eternal Gospel (Phillips translates it 'the *everlasting* Gospel') offering it to every race and nation. This is the supreme mission of the Church in every age – to proclaim this good news, to invite all to hear and respond. But this invitation of the Apocalypse is not sugary, sentimental, superficial. There is something awesome about approaching the God who made all things and is still involved in the making of all that is. '*Reverence God*, and give glory to Him'. There is a solemn grandeur about the Christian religion. Men and women who have been the most effective witnesses to its truth have been like the faithful French preachers at the court of the King of France. It is said that one French preacher startled the noble lords and ladies gathered for the funeral service of a dead king, by crying: 'Only God is great!'

'Give glory to Him' means more. It is like saying: 'Let's celebrate His glory!' The glory of God is His greatness in wisdom, in power, in goodness, in justice, in truth, in beauty, in holiness: above all, in love.

Today we celebrate the Lord's Supper, not only do we perform 'publicly and with due form' this rite, this symbolic representation of the Last Supper Jesus had with His first followers. We celebrate, we show forth, so much of what Christ and His Good News mean.

*First, we celebrate, we give glory to God that He gave us Christ.*

In Christ we see what God is like and what men and women, boys and girls, of every race, nation, class may become. We say: 'Thanks be to God for His unsurpassed gift of Jesus Christ.' Said George Matheson, the sightless but insightful poet-preacher: 'Son of Man, whenever I doubt of life, I think of Thee. Thou never growest old to me. Last century is old. Last year is obsolete fashion. But Thou art not obsolete. Thou art abreast of all the centuries, and I have never come up to Thee, modern as I am.'

*Secondly, we celebrate the glory of God's love which Christ embodied and which finds strange and life-changing focus in the death of Jesus on the Cross.*

The Cross is saying to us, if we could receive it: 'God loves like that.' Love identifies itself with the loved one, suffers to deliver the loved one from all that hurts, degrades, destroys. This love is for all the world. 'God loved the world so much,' says St John, 'that He gave His only Son, that every one who has faith in Him may not die but have eternal life' (John 3$^{16}$, NEB). We celebrate this love, this many splendoured-love, when we take the bread and wine of Holy Communion. Recall St Paul's statement: 'For as often as you eat this bread and drink the cup, you proclaim the Lord's death till He comes' (1 Corinthians 11$^{26}$). You show forth this death for love's sake; you eat proclaiming that God loved you so much that in Christ He died for you.

*Thirdly, we celebrate our forgiveness.*

Says the old-fashioned and beautiful hymn:

> *He died that we might be forgiven,*
> *He died to make us good,*
> *That we might go at last to heaven,*
> *Saved by His precious blood.*

Don't be put off by that phrase 'saved by His precious blood' – to the ancients blood symbolized life. This death was life poured out that we might be saved, healed, made whole again. There is no gain except through pain, no life except through death. Lift up your hearts that God thinks you valuable enough to have Christ suffer and die for you.

*Fourthly, we celebrate the tremendous fact that we are* – as the prayer in our Book of Common Worship and in many another prayer book declares – *'members of the mystical Body of Thy Son, the blessed company of all faithful people and heirs of Thine everlasting Kingdom'*.

On World-wide Communion Sunday we celebrate the reality and world-encircling hope of the society. In Christ's Body all true believers are one. We are all brothers and sisters in Christ. Like most brothers and sisters we differ, dispute, argue, even at times dislike each other. But the more we are 'in Christ' the more we are in this glorious company. 'Now you are the Body of Christ.' *Now!* – not when we resolve all our differences, achieve union and merge into one great organization – we are His Body. Don't translate into a vague future tense what we are offered now, what we possess now. One of the gifts God offers us is our unity in Christ. Let's celebrate our membership in the true catholic Church today.

*Lastly, let's celebrate the fact that because of God's grace we have passed from death into life.*

Physical death is yet to come, but what's that to one who knows that 'He is able to subdue all things to Himself', that 'He is able to keep that which I have committed unto Him against that day?' This Eucharist, this Thanksgiving Service, this Sacrament, needs no Dead March, but the Hallelujah Chorus. With trumpet voice the Sacrament proclaims: 'Death is swallowed up in victory.' 'Christ and you shall live and love when the stars have passed away.'

Dr Robert N. Rodenmayer describes a window in a

great Christian edifice. In Washington Cathedral there is a window designed by a contemporary artist. It is done in the modern manner, stylistically and in bold colours. 'The central scene is the Crucifixion, the offering up of the one life for all lives, and there is no doubt about the fact. But the rest of the scene is also illuminating. Several children of different races and nations are peering out from behind the Cross and their faces are radiant with joy. They look as if they were inviting the onlookers to a picnic, as if they were saying: "You can't kill us because we have already died. We are free to love because we have accepted our death and our resurrection. The battle is over: come to the picnic".'

Let's celebrate!

# ON EXPLAINING EVERYTHING

## David H. C. Read

*Three things are too wonderful for me;*
*four I do not understand:*
*the way of an eagle in the sky,*
*the way of a serpent on a rock,*
*the way of a ship on the high seas,*
*and the way of a man with a maiden.*

Proverbs $30^{18-19}$(RSV)

'Too wonderful for me . . . I do not understand.' Poor
fellow! He lived so long ago. He never heard of aero-
dynamics, biological mutations, astro-physics, chrom-
osomes and genes. Everything was mystery to him. It
was wonderful, because he couldn't understand. Now
that we know all about it, now that we have 'come of
age' (as the 'in-theologians' never tire of telling us),
wouldn't you like to take this primitive Bible writer by
the hand and explain these four things that bothered
him?

'The way of an eagle in the sky?' There's nothing
wonderful about that. You see, it's all a question of
air-displacement. Given the weight of the bird and the
span of the wings, a relatively slight lateral motion of
the latter will suffice to counteract the pull of gravity,
while speed, elevation, and direction are achieved by
appropriate muscular adjustments. As a primitive

154

heavier-than-air mechanism, however, the eagle has been long out-classed in speed and efficiency by human artifacts such as the rocket and the jet-plane – which I don't understand any more than you, but somebody does: so there's no mystery about them.

While the author of these words from the Book of Proverbs is recovering from this, you go on:

'The way of a serpent on a rock?' I see your difficulty. No legs; no wings! How does he move? Elementary zoology would soon explain that for you. 'Locomotion is effected' (I quote) 'by the passage of a series of waves from before backwards, each wave in its progress pressing against the surrounding medium and forcing the animal forwards.' If you still don't understand, I could add that 'the scales of the lower surface are en-larged to form transverse, overlapping plates, whose free edge is directed backwards, and to each of these plates is attached a pair of movable ribs.' You see, microscopes have shown us a lot of things you didn't know about. I could go on to tell you more about the serpent than you would ever want to know. Your problem about the rock, for instance – how does it move on such a smooth surface? Well, it has about three hundred central shields, each of which can utilize any slight irregularity ( I quote again) so 'that progress is possible over almost any surface that is not absolutely smooth'. You see? There's nothing wonderful about the serpent on the rock. We can explain.

Next question?

Ah, yes: 'the way of a ship on the high seas'. I suppose your difficulty is in understanding how the little tub keeps afloat in a storm, and how it ever picks its way across the ocean to the desired harbour. I seem to remember your colleagues who wrote the Book of Psalms having a similar difficulty. 'They that go down to the sea in ships, that do business in great waters: these see the works of the Lord, and His wonders in the deep.' But you don't need to see any wonders or works of the Lord. Even in your day the science of navigation can explain how your little sailing-ship gets from hither to yon. Now we have the whole business so under control that a floating hotel of eighty thousand tons can speed through the high seas with an automatic pilot doing all the steering, and radar doing all the seeing. There's no mystery about it. You and I may not understand it all – but someone does.

Now what was the last thing you mentioned?

'The way of a man with a maiden'? Too wonderful? You don't understand? Now, really, if there's one area where we've made great strides recently it's this business of sex. You primitive people made such a mystery of it, with your rites and ceremonies, your poems and music, your romantic illusions. We've now finally analysed this man-woman relationship. We know all about the biological impulses behind it and we are applying psychological methods to determine its function in society. We are on our way to rationalizing the sex act, and are developing computers to match the right man with the right maiden. A recent book, based on an elaborate investigation under clinical conditions of the way of a man with a maiden, shows the way towards a complete understanding of human sexuality. You won't need to wonder any more. You'll understand. You'll know all about it.

Well, is this how you really feel? Let's begin by being quite realistic. We do know immensely more about the physical world than the Bible writers. We do know more about the nature of the universe, the transmission of life, the mastery of the elements, the functioning of the human body and psyche. The advance of human knowledge has been extraordinary since the Bible was written and never more so than in the last fifty years. The understanding that modern science has given us, and the benefits it has conferred, are beyond computing. My old teacher, Dr H. R. Mackintosh, Professor of Dogmatics at Edinburgh University, used to warn us that a preacher never looks more foolish than when he starts attacking the scientist. The liberating spirit of inquiry has brought mankind to a new era in the conquest of hunger and disease, and in the control of the forces of nature. And this understanding has been gained at great price, for science has its martyrs as well as religion.

My purpose in this sermon is simply to raise a huge question-mark over against the idea that our scientific understanding of things is sufficient and complete, and that therefore we have arrived at a point in the human story when wonder, mystery, the intuitions of the mystic, the vision of the artist, the realm of the spirit, can all be ruled out as avenues of truth and guides for the human mind. The point is not that there are still some things that science cannot explain. He would be a bold man who rested the case for religion on the gaps in the scientific picture today. I am confident that science will go on exploring and investigating in every area, even those we used to think belonged only to morals and religions. The Bible itself suggests no 'Keep Out' sign for the inquiring mind. What we have to ask is whether this kind of explanation – even if it covered the sum total of human experience – really offers, or ever can offer, any answer to the ultimate questions that concern us all. We don't just want to know 'How': we want to know 'Why'. You can explain to me to the limit of my capacity the complexities of the atom, the cellular structure of life, the rhythm of the solar system, the sweep of the galaxies through the infinities of time and space, but I am asking :'What does it mean? Is there anything behind this process?' We are told today that such questions are foolish: they are a sign of middle age. Yet I find them raised, in one form or another, by every student group I meet in discussion. The search for meaning lies behind the eruption of demonstrations, new trends in music, dance, poetry, drama – and even fashion. It is as though a generation to whom everything is in process of being explained has realized that ultimately nothing has been explained at all. There are other ways of listening to the universe. The telescope and micro-scope are not the only windows into truth.

There was a time when the religious believer was accused of a narrow mind. And there are indeed religious people who live in a little chamber of piety from which they glare suspiciously at the ways of the modern world. Churches in the past have too often obstructed the path of science, neglected the contribution of the arts and fostered a timid and negative attitude to life. But I suspect that we may now be reaching the point where it is the thorough-going secularist, the dogmatic rationalist, who is being revealed as narrow-minded. To limit one's convictions to that which is capable of scientific explanation, to attempt to reduce every vivid experience to computer-fodder, to interpret the religious and moral insights of the human race in terms of subjective emotion, is narrow-minded dogmatism – a deliberate exclusion of a whole dimension of existence. A revolt against this secularist fundamentalism is now under way – and that brings me back to the eagle, the serpent, the ship on the high seas, and the way of a man with a maiden.

Let's leave the snorting, swirling city for a moment and dream ourselves off to some distant mountain peak, where we sit on a rock, looking out over a sea of peaks coloured by the glinting sun as the clouds drift by. And here comes the eagle, hovering, swooping, soaring, and gliding off into a distant speck on the far horizon. Are we sitting there thinking of aero-dynamics? Are we at that moment any wiser than the Bible writer who found the way of an eagle in the sky too wonderful for him? Is what the artist sees as he catches the curve and flight, even of a common seagull, not more important to us than a mountain of statistical research? Can the moment of wonder not open a window for us into a dimension of mystery and of God that has more meaning than a wilderness of factual information?

I do not understand. Feed me all the information that is tucked away in a thousand microfilms, and I still stand here and wonder. And I wonder about the serpent on the rock. I listen to the strange voices of the past that come hissing through the collective unconsciousness of mankind. There is the primeval symbol of temptation; there is the healing snake lifted high on a pole; there is the legend of the sea-serpent; there is the trail of the serpent through the imagery of our dreams; there is the poison, the elusive-ness, the cunning; there is Cleopatra that 'serpent of old Nile'. The window opens into a strange world, where there are hopes and fears, shapes of good and evil, and at such a moment God can speak. Never to be transfixed by one single living creature – a serpent on a rock, an ant carrying its eggs, a fly moving on the window-pane, or the sheer improbability of a hippopotamus, is to be terribly impoverished. There are times when we don't want to know the facts. We just wonder. Tell me, do we really *understand* any more what it all means than the man who wrote these Proverbs long ago?

That ship on the high seas – what was it that roused him to wonder and amazement? I don't think it was the technical achievement. He probably knew quite a lot about sails and rudders, tides and winds. I believe he was suddenly seized with the thought that comes to us all: 'Why?' Why has the earth-bound, two-legged creature called man the desire to cut down trees and make a ship? Why does he entrust himself to the dark and menacing ocean? Where is he going, and why does he want to go? For us exactly the same questions come surging in when we see a capsule off into space containing another of these our fellowmen. For the achievement we have all the explanations – if we can follow them. There is no mystery about the calculations, the experiments, the years of research, that have preceded the launching that we watch. The mystery, the wonder, the confession that we do not understand, come with our deeper questions. What strange compulsion has led man to this mastery of his environment? What, if anything, lies behind the evolution of such a creature on this earth? Where is he going, and why does he want to go? Last summer I stopped at a drug-store in Pennsylvania. Behind the counter on a television set was the picture of a space-shot and we heard the voices of two astronauts as they sped around the earth at eighteen thousand miles per hour. The assistant was leaning on the counter discussing with a customer a minor traffic accident that had just happened in the village. So soon these astonishing achievements are taken for granted. Just because we know what can be done and can guess perhaps at more to come, must we lose all sense of wonder? Are we going to become the race of people who understand everything – and therefore understand nothing? Or can we still say about the mystery of man's existence and his questioning spirit 'too wonderful for me. . . I do not understand'?

Last week *Life* magazine published a letter from a lady concerning the book called *Human Sexual Response*. She said her reaction was to plead for a 'Society for the Preservation of the Sweet Mystery of Life'. Amen! All right, let's have the facts. There has been certainly too much ignorance and hush-hush about sex in the past. But what kind of life awaits a people for whom the way of man with a maiden is entirely explainable in terms of glands and genes and psychological data? The Bible is plain enough about the mere facts of sex, but the way of a man with a maiden is also seen in the dimension of wonder and mystery. The Song of Songs is there as well as the sex laws of the Pentateuch. Into what drab world are we moving when sheer explanation takes over, and wonder and poetry disappear?

> *O, my Luve's like a red, red rose*
> *That's newly sprung in June:*
> *O, my Luve's like a melodie*
> *That's sweetly played in tune.*

Must we now learn to sing:

> *O, my Luve's like a chromosome*
> *That seeks the perfect suitor:*
> *And my Luve will be chosen for me*
> *By some great big computer?*

The preservation of mystery, the revival of a sense of wonder, the recognition of a dimension in life that cannot be explained away – these alone will make a man or woman a Christian. And I am not suggesting that just because there is still wonder and mystery therefore you must be prepared to accept everything the Church has to say about the being of God, the person of Christ or the work of the Holy Spirit. I am just telling you how not to close the door. That is all the Book of Proverbs is doing. But it is immensely important to free ourselves from the tyranny of over-explanation, the shackles of a dogmatic secularism. It pervades the atmosphere we breathe and can follow us even into church. We tend to want our worship rationalized and all our beliefs explained. We have been losing the sense of mystery and the sheer joy of saying: 'Lord, I believe; but I do not understand.' 'Worship,' said Thomas Carlyle, 'is transcendent wonder.' In the Book of the Acts you find the early Church glowing with the sense of transcendent wonder. They offered their explanations; they argued and expounded; they organized and campaigned; but through it all rang the note of utter astonishment at what they called 'the wondrous works of God'.

We are moving to the season when the Church is reminded of the presence and work of the Holy Spirit.

One way in which the Spirit moves is in the opening of the windows of the soul, the preparation for the vision of Christ. We are very much aware today of the secular obligations of the Christian, of the necessity for the Church to be present and active in human affairs. We are continuously engaged in the work of explanation – explaining our doctrines, our worship, our activities. Should we not also be giving our attention to that inner realm where the good news of Jesus Christ presses in upon us with an authority that cannot be explained, where the glory of God is revealed in the flight of an eagle, the twist of a serpent, the adventure into space, the way of a man with a maiden? Worship is the transcendent wonder of men and women who know that life is more than maps and measurement, data and statistics, timetables and graphs. Christian worship is our wonder and amazement at the gift of God in Jesus Christ our Lord, our openness to the presence and power of the Holy Spirit and our glimpse of the world unseen through such simple elements as water, bread, and wine. These things are too wonderful for me. I do not understand. But through them you and I may find the gift that alone can satisfy the soul – 'the peace of God that passeth *all* understanding'.

# SHEPHERD, GUIDE AND HOST

## William Graham Scroggie

### Psalm 23

The twenty-third Psalm is, surely, the most beautiful flower that grows in the garden of sacred poetry. It is the sweetest songster of all the melody-makers of the forest. It has been called 'the Shepherd Psalm'; but we shall see, I hope, that it is a great deal more than that.

The language of it compels us to see several figures here. I hold that in this poem there are three figures. You have, first, *the Shepherd and the Sheep;* then you have *the Guide and the Traveller.* You see the traveller being led in the paths of righteousness, and having of necessity to go through the valley of the shadow of death, but not fearing because his Guide has a rod and a staff with which to protect him. And you have also *the Host and the Guest* – the figure of hospitality. You have three perfect figures blended, and that which gives unity to the whole psalm is the fact that the Lord and the soul stand in these relations to one another.

*Let us take the Shepherd and the Sheep.*

There you have provision. The sheep is known chiefly for its wants, and they are few and simple. The sheep wants good pasture and good water, it wants to eat and it wants to drink; and, when it stops doing that, it wants to sleep.

Well, here it is. 'He maketh me to lie down in green pastures; He leadeth me beside the still waters.' The sheep can lie down in pastures of tender grass, and eat to its satisfaction; and then the shepherd leads it beside the waters of quietness and of rest.

So you get the grass and the brook, food and drink, and the shepherd looking after the wants of the sheep.

The only Shepherd referred to in the New Testament is Christ. There are many references to shepherds in the Old Testament. Christ is called the 'good', the 'great' and the 'chief' Shepherd; and that good and that great and that chief Shepherd is my Shepherd, too; and I shall not want. He knows where the tender grass is; He knows where the babbling brook runs; and He will find me a quiet resting place.

*Pass now to the Guide and the Traveller.*

Provision is not all that we need in this life. We are sheep only in one aspect, and that aspect does not cover the whole of life. And so the figure changes, and instead of the Shepherd we have the Guide; and instead of being sheep, we find that we are pilgrims, and we have got to travel.

What is the need of the pilgrim? Let us follow the psalm again. 'He restoreth my soul.' That means that he turns my soul back to the starting point. Have you ever lost your way toward nightfall on a trackless moor? I know of nothing more bewildering when the shadows of evening are gathering thick, and the night is coming on apace, than to be lost on a mountainside or on a moor. What do we need at such a time? We need a guide. What to do? To turn us back to the starting point, to put us right, and that is what this Guide does. He turns my soul back to the starting point. And how does He do it? By leading me in the paths of righteousness, by conducting me along the right track! He puts my feet in the right way. And why does He do it? Because He has a reputation: it is 'for His name's sake'.

There are people in business who, having been successful, wish to sell it; and they sell the goodwill of their name, so that the old name might be kept above the door when the business has passed into the hands of someone else. The name is too good to lose, and those who buy the business have to pay for the name, because the name stands for a reputation.

So the Lord's name stands for His nature; and when He turns a soul that has gone astray back to the starting point and puts the feet of that one on the right track, in the way of righteousness, He is doing it, not only for the sake of the individual but for His own name's sake, for His reputation's sake.

And the way in which He leads us may lie where we least would have it. 'Yea (*moreover* – that's what it means) though I walk through the valley of the shadow of death, I will fear no evil, for Thou art with me.' That is commonly interpreted as referring to the end of life, but it is not so. It is 'the valley of the shadow of death', or, more literally, 'gloomy ravine', 'the valley of deep darkness'. Where you have mountains on both sides how deep is the darkness in the valley and how cold it is there! For the most part, it is a fearsome gorge: yet that does not refer to the end but to the whole of life. 'Yea, though I walk, as I must, through the valley which is filled with gloom and across the ravine that is dark, I will not fear.' Why? Because 'Thou art with me.' What does it matter so long as the Lord is with us? A little child is not afraid so long as he feels the grip of his father's, or his mother's, hand.

It is the companion that makes the journey. We are sheep, and we need a Shepherd. We are travellers, and we need a Guide.

*But there is more. Turn now, finally, to the Host and the Guest.*

These three figures, seeing that the psalm was written by David, would seem to reflect three of his own experiences. David began his life as a shepherd boy on the hillside. Then, you remember, later he became a fugitive. Saul hated him and tried to kill him; and so David had to flee for his life and he became a fugitive and lived in caves and in holes in the mountainside. And there you get the next figure – that of the Guide and the Traveller. Afterwards David came to the throne; he became a king and had a palace, and he entertained guests. His enemies had tried to kill him but they did not succeed. 'Thou preparest a table before me in the presence of mine enemies.' They had hunted and pursued him, but the moment he got over the threshold of the palace he was safe: they could not enter into the palace, and so they stood around glowering and grumbling. How tantalizing for David's enemies to see him having a good time at the table and they not allowed to cross the threshold!

I would call your attention to the word 'enemies' here. It is the same word from which we get the words 'Czar', 'Caesar', 'Kaiser'. It means 'to cramp', 'to limit'. In these designations we have the thought of the assumption of power over the individual, such as no one should have. We have seen it in our time in the dictatorships. Dictators have no regard for the rights of the individual. They are oppressors. They limit and cramp the individual life that God meant to be free *in* Him and *for* Him.

So it says here: 'Thou preparest a table before me in the presence of mine enemies'; in the presence of those who would cramp my life and limit my usefulness. They cannot come across the threshold into Thy house. Thou spreadest before me, Thou settest in order before me a feast, and what a feast! The table creaks beneath the weight of the rich viands which my Host supplies. When I come from the bath to the meal, my Host anoints my head with oil, an Eastern custom of courtesy. And then He takes my cup, and out of the decanter He fills it to the brim, and then He puts in more until it runs over.

But I cannot sit at the table all the time: there are my enemies there, waiting. What is to be done? 'Surely goodness and mercy shall follow me all the days of my life.'

You know that in the stories of the classics gods and goddesses were appointed tasks. Some were enemies and some were friends; some guarded, some destroyed. But my Host is not going to let me go over that threshold into the outer world alone. Goodness and Mercy – two of His servants – are called to follow the guest and do anything for him that he may need. Goodness and Mercy, my two attendants, shall follow me all the days of my life. They will consider my wants. They will defend and protect me along the whole path of life right up to death; and then, as to the other side of death, why,

'I will dwell in the House of the Lord for ever.' The Delectable House up there in the mountains that John Bunyan speaks about in his *Pilgrim's Progress*, the shining Host to greet me after every tortuous way has been trodden, after every fearsome enemy has been faced and overcome, after every dark ravine has been traversed. Yes, at the end, the House of the Lord for ever.

The sheep needs the Shepherd, the traveller needs the Guide, the guest needs the Host. And the Shepherd and the Guide and the Host are all one – the Lord, the Creator of all. He knows the dangers that threaten the sheep; He knows the darkness and the coldness of that deep gorge, for He went there before me to make a bridle-track for me, and I see blood-drops all along the way.

But He did not perish in the gorge, and I shall not. He brings me to His eternal Home, where the light never fades and the music never ceases.

This lovely twenty-third Psalm! Read it! Memorize it! Repeat it every day! Make it you own! Get to know your Shepherd, your Guide and your Host!

> *The King of Love my Shepherd is,*
> *Whose goodness faileth never;*
> *I nothing lack if I am His*
> *And He is mine for ever.*

From *The Christian World*, 23 February 1939

# THE WATER OF THE WELL AT BETHLEHEM

## GORDON S. WAKEFIELD

*And David said longingly: 'Oh, that someone would give me water to drink from the well of Bethlehem which is by the gate!' Then the three mighty men broke through the camp of the Philistines, and drew out of the well of Bethlehem which was by the gate, and took it and brought it to David. But he would not drink of it; he poured it out to the Lord, and said: 'Far be it from me, O Lord, that I should do this. Shall I drink the blood of the men who went at risk of their lives?' Therefore he would not drink it.*
2 Samuel 23[15]

A great many of us come to David's position in this story. I am not thinking of the dangers by which he was surrounded, though Plato said that we are all like dwellers in a cave, and we know well that we are besieged by enemies of the soul. I am thinking, rather, of his *longing*. Though in momentary peril of the Philistines, he is a man of destiny, fame and power, on whose brow has been poured the sacred oil dedicating him to kingship. Yet he craves for the water of the well of Bethlehem, which he had known as a boy; which symbolizes the solace of human comfort, and particularly our desire to have in the present, which may be even more conspicuous or successful than the past, those warm and homely relationships from which time and change have separated us.

David desires more than victory and a throne, more in this moment than some opportunity of serving God. He wants the water of the well of Bethlehem. And so do most of us.

Any company of people contains men and women of different persuasions and temperaments. There may be so-called supermen without the common feelings of humanity, victors over every passion, disinterested in food and drink and sex and pleasure and friendship. There may be people almost devoid of desires, cold and passionless, who do not know the pangs of longing. But if you were given the choice between fame and human love, between making what men call 'history' and knowing the homely joys, which would you prefer? The purple-filled goblet of success and service, or the water of the well of Bethlehem? And this cup is so often dashed from our hands! Sometimes, indeed, it must be repudiated for the sake of vocation. But, often enough, it is circumstances which deprive us of it.

Edward Grey was Foreign Secretary in the Asquith government at the outbreak of the First World War. He it was who spoke about the lamps going out all over Europe. He himself did not seek the eminence of power. He hated Westminster and was never happier than when he was in his native Northumberland enjoying the delights of the countryside. He wanted to escape from politics and to find refuge in home and family. Yet twice he was tragically bereaved and left childless.

There are some to whom unsatisfied desires are a real problem. It is this which makes youth so difficult. In Plato's *Republic* an old man, named Cephalus, welcomes old age because it brings peace and freedom from the passions, 'masters many and ravening'. This may not be true of all the aged, as he was aware.

One of the greatest problems for pastors and psychiatrists is that of the woman who has been denied children. I have known at least one who could never bear to join in baptismal services because of the heartache at the thought of her own deprivation.

Admittedly, those of us who desire passionately human joys may become just sentimental. We may indulge in a luxury of emotion without action. There is some satisfaction in sighing when we ought to be active. Unsatisfied desires can be as a fire in the bones, but also as a fire by which we warm ourselves and perhaps deny Christ.

But the Gospel recognizes these longings. There is that in it which is a shock to the austere. . . 'The Son of Man came eating and drinking'. And unless we had these human longings, we should be incapable of love and sacrifice. The true martyr does not desire martyrdom but other things, and yet counts these loss for Christ. These three mighty men were of the same psychological type as David—they would not have gone through the Philistine hosts unless they had understood his longing and themselves yearned for his friendship. Passionless hearts would never venture as they did in the service of love. But it is David's action which concerns us most.

*First, he recognized what it really was that the three men brought back to him.* 'Shall I drink the blood of these men who went in jeopardy of their lives?'

I suppose that some would have demanded that he submit the water to chemical analysis. The late Bishop of Birmingham suggested that such an experiment be carried out to test the validity of the Presence of Christ in the bread and wine of the Sacrament. But does not such a request reveal a mind somewhat deficient in spiritual sensitiveness and understanding? True, there have been those within the faith equally prosaic who have regarded the elements of Holy Communion with a literal and carnal devotion – though the Roman dogma of Transubstantiation (change of the substance of the bread and wine) is not so crude, nor so grievous, an error as some have thought it to be. I am not convinced that this by itself would be enough to separate us from Rome. But it may be that we can interpret Christ's words over bread and cup by this story. David was speaking neither as scientist nor philosopher, but the water was changed into blood for him.

And does not this imply a wider sacramentalism? Is anything merely what is seems to be when examined by the five senses? No blessing of life is trivial, not even the most homely. You are not wanting a little thing if you wish for the joys of human love and friendship, a house to live in and bread to eat.

A remarkable Christian literary man of this century, Charles Williams, felt that there was a history of pain implied in each element of common life or household task.

*Bathing or lighting a fire or going downstairs,*
*What old companions crowd, see, in our first need!*

Whenever he washed his hands or struck a match, he would remember those who had perished by water or fire.

And it is one of the lessons of life that all the gifts of God are mediated through sacrifice. So often we take as a right and without reverence that which has only been bought by the groaning and travail of the whole creation. And surely it is the crudest and grossest of all errors to think that we have any rights, or that we ourselves have earned or deserved any temporal blessing. And if our eyes were opened we should see something of the pattern of Christ's Cross everywhere – of His great Sacrifice.

> *I see His blood upon the rose*
> *And in the stars the glory of His eyes;*
> *His body gleams amid eternal snows,*
> *His tears fall from the skies.*

> *All pathways by His feet are worn,*
> *His strong heart stirs the ever-beating sea;*
> *His crown of thorns is twined with every thorn,*
> *His Cross is every tree.*

*But, secondly, David did more than see the significance of the gift. He offered it to God.*

All the joys and blessings of earth, all human love and sacrifice, the satisfaction of all our desires are for the worship of God. The world of nature, of which we form a part, is given us not so much that we may find God in it as offer it to Him. The passionate love of men and women consummated in marriage is not a delectable way of propagating the species, much less an opportunity for delirious self-indulgence. It is a means for the worship of God, 'signifying unto us the mystical union between Christ and His Church'. These things are not ends in themselves: they point us to God and demand their fulfilment in Him.

That is what the Christian religion seeks to do by the first and last offices of our holy religion, baptism and burial. When we bring a baby to enter into the benefits of Christ's passion through the sprinkling of water, we offer him to God. But have you ever thought that we do just this at a funeral? The same hymn of Philip Doddridge would almost serve for both rites.

> *We bring them, Lord, with thankful hands*
> *And yield them up to Thee.*

And if the water of the well of Bethlehem seems to be snatched from him the Christian is not content merely to be deprived – he seeks to make even the cruellest loss an offering to God.

A. J. Gossip has told of a Scotsman and his wife who had to watch their little daughter die, but the father said to the mother: 'We will not let her be taken from us, we will give her freely.' And if sometimes it seems as if the water is poured into the dry ground and lost for ever, we believe that it has, in fact, run into the imperishable springs of eternity and 'God seeketh again that which is passed away.'

*But, finally, there may be something else in the story. Perhaps David offered the water to God not only out of humility before the love of his friends or in understanding that it was given for Divine worship, but because he knew he was not worthy to drink it.*

We need more than the satisfaction of our desires – we need salvation from sin; more than refreshment – cleansing.

You see, this nostalgia for the past and its relationships is not for any actual state of our lives on earth.
Would David have been satisfied to have been a boy,
again playing at the well of Bethlehem and quenching
his summer thirst from it? It may well appear as a
yearning for what we have 'loved long since and lost
awhile', but we have not lost it simply by the passing
of the years, or because our childhood has gone. It is
part of the frustration and tragedy of the race. And,
to deliver us, we need more than our own efforts or the
comradeship of our friends.

There was an eminent Oxford scholar of last century,
named Richard William Church. For twenty years in
his prime he was rector of the little Somerset village of
Whatley near Frome. Then they made him Dean of
St Paul's Cathedral. And it is generally recognized that
of all that long line of eminent churchmen whose works
have enriched our land, he was the greatest. Yet his
heart never left Whatley. He often must have craved
for the water of its well. And when he died, he who
could have had a tomb in his own cathedral, insisted
that he be taken back to the village churchyard. And
they laid him in the shelter of the church walls between
the chancel and the south transept, and they put, at
his instruction, the Latin of these words on the simple
stone:

> *Faint and weary Thou hast sought me,*
> *On the Cross of suffering bought me:*
> *Shall such grace be vainly brought me?*

You see, there was another Boy who was born in
Bethlehem, who Himself grew up and delighted in the

pleasures and comforts of human life, laughter and the love of friends. But these were all taken from Him. And yet, though apparently His enemies overcame Him, He Himself advanced through their hosts, and brings us the chalice of His most precious blood.

The Fourth Evangelist records that after Jesus had died they pierced His side with a lance. 'And there came out from the side of Jesus blood and water.'

There is little doubt that in his mystical, allusive way St John refers to the two great Christian sacraments of Communion and Baptism, which symbolize both the satisfaction of our desires and the cleansing of our sins in Christ. And as we advance in our pilgrimage another need will increasingly be added to the longing of our nature. We shall not only desire to drink the water of human love become wine in God's Kingdom. We shall pray with the unknown medieval saint:

*Water from the side of Christ wash me.*

There was a cantankerous little clergyman who lived in eighteenth-century England. He was always involved in theological controversies and arid debates and used the most opprobrious language to defend his opinions. He once indeed called John Wesley 'a mean and puny tadpole in divinity', which the founder of Methodism certainly was not. One of this writer's most turgid works is a treatise which begins with the national debt and then, after pages of economics, goes on to apply the bankrupt state of the nation to the human soul, saying that we, too, are all paupers before God. But, at the end of his uninspired paragraphs, there follows this poem:

'A Living and Dying Prayer for the Holiest Believer
   in the World'

> *Rock of Ages, cleft for me,*
> *Let me hide myself in Thee;*
> *Let the water and the blood,*
> *From Thy riven side which flowed,*
> *Be of sin the double cure,*
> *Cleanse me from its guilt and power.*

And that *is* 'a living and dying prayer for the *holiest*
believer in the world'!